Old Windows In-Depth

The Complete Window Restoration Handbook

By Scott Sidler

Copyright 2018 Austin Enterprises

INTRODUCTION

In 2015 when I wrote Old Windows Made Easy, I wanted to give homeowners a step by step plan to restore their windows themselves. Since then, I have sold thousands of books all over the world and more windows are being saved from the landfill than ever before.

It's a great feeling knowing that a simple little book like that could save so many historic windows. I tried to leave out so much of the theory and history that other window books were filled with. I felt that it got in the way and distracted from the task at hand, which of course is taking old windows and making them new again.

Don't get me wrong, the why, history, and backstory of what's involved in the process of window restoration is important. Important enough that I have read dozens of books to learn as much as I can about the details of these old windows. I just feel that there are other folks with a more exacting nature who have written comprehensive tomes on historic windows that are better suited as sources for this information.

My strength has always been a laser focus on "doing" and I wanted a book that helped people take action right away and not get bogged down in the theory.

After publishing Old Windows Made Easy, I knew that I was leaving some things out. Things that people would want to know how to do, but I didn't feel that it needed to be included in the base level book. That book was never intended to be comprehensive because of the sheer variety of windows out there from centuries of different craftsmen forming their windows according to local traditions.

Every region had its own way of doing things. Uniquely routed profiles, different species of wood, scores of unique balance systems from ropes to tapes to springs. The list of different features goes on and on.

Can any one book contain EVERYTHING you need to know about old windows? It's doubtful. With the first book, I tried to cover the basic processes and order of operations to give you the simplest way to restore a wood window. With this book, I'm filling in the blanks. All of the potential problems that might occur, but don't always rear their ugly heads. Old Windows In-Depth gives you all of the ammunition that you need in the fight to restore.

What's Inside

In part one of this book, you'll get a revised version of the full text of Old Windows Made Easy to get you rolling. Then, in part two, you'll find over a hundred pages of new tutorials and information about restoring windows covering topics like weatherstripping options, advanced sash repair techniques, tutorials on storm and screen making, glass and paint options and techniques, even a full section on the complete process of restoring steel windows!

Double-hung windows are the most typical windows in most parts of the country, but there are other styles of windows that you may encounter like casement, awning, and steel windows, and so, I've included restoration techniques and tips for all of these types of windows and more.

A lot of the chapters in this book came from suggestions from readers like you. The more often I got requests for additional tutorials, the more likely I was to include them in this follow up book. So, you can consider this book the "old windows request hour" where I answer your questions.

Just like the original book, all of the information here will be in easy to follow, step-by-step tutorials to help you not just understand what needs to get done, but to get to work on it today.

This book will hopefully serve to fill in the blanks for those of you dealing with unique window setups and answer a lot of the questions I get every week. Most importantly, there is minimal theory and conjecture, just time tested, step-by-step restoration techniques to walk you through the process. Enough lead in, let's get into the tutorials so that you can start restoring your windows right now!

TABLE OF CONTENTS

INTRODUCTION	2
PART 1	9
TAKING BACK PRESERVATION	10
6 Myths About Old Windows	12
WINDOW BASICS	15
How to Use This Guide	15
Small Victories	15
Wood, Putty & Glass	16
Window Anatomy	17
SAFETY FIRST	20
Lead Paint	20
Asbestos	20
Lead Safe Work Practices	21
Setup & Cleanup	21
PPE (Personal Protective Equipment)	23
Low-Dust Work Techniques	24
MECHANICAL RESTORATION	25
Prep	26

Remove Interior Stop	28
Remove Bottom Sash	30
Remove Parting Bead	32
Remove Top Sash	34
Rope Removal	36
Rope Installation	38
Finishing up	40

JAMB RESTORATION — 41

Jamb Paint Removal	42
Jamb Wood Repair	44
Jamb Priming & Painting	46
Parting Bead & Stop	48
Cover Openings	50

HARDWARE RESTORATION — 52

Pulley Restoration	53
Hardware Restoration	54
Aging Hardware	56

SASH RESTORATION — 58

Paint Removal	60
Deglazing	62
Dutchman Repairs	64
Epoxy Repairs	66

Sand & Prep	68
Priming	70
Glass Prep	72
Bed Glass	74
Finish Glaze	76
Finish Painting	78
Re-install Top Sash	80
Re-install Bottom Sash	82

PART II — 84
WORKING WITH VARNISHED WINDOWS — 86

Changing to a Painted Finish	86
Restoring a Natural Finish	87

WEATHERSTRIPPING OPTIONS — 92
INSTALLING & REMOVING WEATHERSTRIPPING — 95

How to Install Spring Bronze	95
Curved Installation of Spring Bronze	98
Working with Integrated Metal	99

REPAIRING & REPLACING SUBSILLS — 104

Integrated SubSills	104
Separate SubSills	106

CASEMENTS, AWNINGS & HOPPERS, OH MY! — 109

Casement Windows	109

    Awning Windows   111

    Hopper Windows   114

    Single Hung Windows   115

CHAINS, ROPES, & WEIGHTS   119

    Chain or Rope?   119

    Working with Sash Weights   121

    Cutting Weight Pockets   123

    4 Hacks for Roping Windows   127

PAINTING OPTIONS   128

    Types of Paints   128

    Using Pre-treatments   129

GLASS OPTIONS   132

STORMS & SCREENS   137

    Exterior Storms   137

    Interior Storms   139

    Making Affordable Screens   140

PUTTY OPTIONS   144

ADVANCED SASH REPAIR   148

    Dutchman Repairs in Depth   148

    Glazing Bar Repairs   150

    Joinery Repairs   153

WORKING WITH STEAM   156

Deglazing with Steam	157
Removing Paint with Steam	158
UNIQUE MECHANICALS	**159**
Spiral Balances	159
Tape Balances	163
Vinyl Jamb Liners	166
Spring Bolts	169
RESTORING STEEL WINDOWS	**170**
Prep	173
Deglazing	174
Paint Removal	175
Glass Prep	176
Rust Treatment and Priming	177
Glass Replacement	178
Glazing	179
Finish Paint	180
Interior Restoration	181
Step 10	183
Hardware Restoration	183
CONCLUSION	**185**
APPENDIX: WINDOW TOOL & SUPPLIES	**187**

PART 1

TAKING BACK PRESERVATION

I've watched too many old windows get ripped out of houses and thrown to the curb over the years. It's a wasteful tragedy that seems to only grow. Every year, there are fewer and fewer of these original windows in our historic buildings.

It's a disturbing trend that has made me and other preservationists feel absolutely powerless in our aims to save America's windows.

My restoration company, like many others, works tirelessly restoring hundreds of old windows every year, but there is only so much that we can do. There is a limit to how many windows our shops can restore in a year. It feels like a losing battle sometimes when I see another house get its original windows replaced with vinyl. One more piece of history in the landfill.

I've finally come to the point where I can't stand on the sidelines and watch anymore. We Americans have been lied to. We have been sold a bill of goods by the replacement window industry, by the Energy Star program, and to some extent, by the very preservation organizations that seek to save these old buildings.

They've convinced us that eco-friendly and efficient mean newer. Preservation groups may fight to save old buildings, but while fighting the good fight I've seen many "admit" that though these old buildings are worth saving, they are not energy-efficient.

What? How is tearing portions of these houses out and throwing them away an efficient use of energy and resources? I understand what they are saying, but I think it's far from helpful.

Yes, after being neglected for years, old windows can leak like a sieve. The weatherstripping is missing in action. The wood is rotting from lack of painting. But, the energy-efficient solution is not to tear it out and put in something new. The solution is to restore it.

- Preserving America's windows is…energy-efficient.
- Preserving America's windows is…NOT the government's job.
- Preserving America's windows is…a worthy goal.
- Preserving America's windows is…our responsibility.
- Preserving America's windows is…something YOU can do.

I'm taking back preservation. Taking it out of the hands of government organizations and preservation professionals, because truthfully, the work we contribute is a drop in the ocean.

While we sit around and congratulate ourselves on the latest piece of history that we've saved, 10 more are quietly torn down and thrown in the landfill.

We have been ineffective at saving America's history, and so, I'm taking it back and giving it to you. You can save our history. You can save our windows. And you can empower your community.

Here's the difference: When I restore a house full of old windows and put my yard sign up, the neighbors usually take note and think, "That company did a very nice job restoring those old windows." (At least that's what I hope they are thinking!) Then they go along with their day thinking nothing much of it. Maybe they call for an estimate and maybe we'll do their windows too, but maybe not.

When you restore your windows, when you take matters into your own hands and your neighbors see it, your friends hear your tales about restoring these pieces of history, your co-workers hear about your weekend exploits with these old windows, it raises a level of awareness that a preservation organization like mine can't match.

Any preservation company is seen as biased in favor of saving old windows. Just like you wouldn't ask the CEO of Ford if he thinks Ford or Chevy makes a better truck.

You know what the answer would be, and even though he could back it up with all kinds of stats and test results, you would take it with a grain of salt because he obviously has an agenda, right? He wants to sell more Ford trucks.

The same goes for preservation. When I talk about saving old windows, people may listen, they may even be interested enough to buy my book, but they usually see me as unfairly biased in favor of old windows and old houses.

When the average homeowner starts talking about why they are choosing to restore their old windows, that's when the community listens. Your circle of friends and neighbors will want to know why and how. Why did you choose to restore instead of replace? How did you learn to do it yourself? Is it even possible to do yourself?

When you answer, they will listen, and this thing called preservation will spread like wildfire throughout the country. The idea will spread at dinners, BBQs, children's parties, nail salons, gyms, grocery stores, anywhere you go and talk to someone about it, you can plant the idea that we can do it ourselves.

If I were to restore all of the old windows in my city, it would take me several lifetimes. I've got a great crew working with me, but even with 20, 40, or even 100 people on staff, we still couldn't get through the workload in this lifetime.

What would happen if everyone decided to restore their own windows? Well, first, I'd be out of a job because in one month's time, every old window would be restored. But, that would be okay with me, because my job is really to save our history. If by writing this book, I can put myself and other preservation tradesmen and women out of business, most of us would celebrate all the way to the unemployment office.

Ultimately, preservation is in your hands if you want it. By buying this book, you've taken the first step in taking back the power to change your community and save America's history.

I don't just want you to restore your old windows, but to feel empowered to take on other projects around your old house. Share this book with neighbors and friends. Be the start of a revitalization in your town, whether you're out in the country or in the big city, you can do it. I'm merely pointing the way.

6 Myths About Old Windows

Lies, lies abound when it comes to old windows. Window companies proclaim how their replacement windows will do everything from curing cancer to saving the whales (hyperbole intended!).

How can you tell if a window salesman is lying? His lips are moving.

There isn't a single part of an old house that is in nearly as much danger of disappearing as old windows. We've been made to believe that they are wasteful, energy hogging, lead encrusted death traps that are beyond saving, but the truth couldn't be more different.

I'll try to dispel some of the myths that I hear from homeowners, contractors, architects, and even some preservationists about why original windows should be replaced.

1. Old windows are inefficient and waste energy

Windows account for only about 10-20% of energy loss in a typical building (much less than attics and roofs). Once restored and weatherstripped properly, single-pane historic windows can exceed the 2012 International Energy Conservation Code (IECC) requirement of 0.2 CFM. Source: Window Preservation Standards 2013 field testing ASTM E783 "Standard Test Method for Field Measurement of Air Leakage Through Installed Exterior Windows and Doors"

And with the addition of exterior storm windows or interior storm panels, they can reach performance of 0.05 CFM or nearly 4 times more efficient than the code requires!

2. Old windows are difficult and costly to repair

Historic windows are actually quite simple to repair. Their parts (sash cord, pulleys, locks, etc.) along with individual glass panes and glazing putty are available locally and designed to be easily replaced or repaired when they reach the end of their useable life.

There are no complex, proprietary parts that may or may not be in production anymore. They can be restored many times over and their lives extended into centuries of use, compared with replacement windows, which have a short and finite lifespan before requiring replacement again and again.

3. Wood rots easily and steel rusts, making them a bad material for windows

Neglect is the number one cause of damage to these old windows. Once restored, historic windows need minimal regular maintenance, but this maintenance can allow them to last decades longer than replacement windows. It's only after years of neglect that problems occur and the costs escalate. Original windows are made from materials like old-growth wood, which is more rot and insect resistant than anything available today.

The workmanship on these windows also surpasses the mechanical connections in replacement windows, being constructed with pegged mortise and tenon joints, which are the strongest and most stable joinery made by Master Carpenters.

4. Old windows always stick and don't operate smoothly and reliably

This comes down to neglected maintenance, once again. The weight and pulley counterbalance system used in most double-hung historic windows has never been improved upon. It provides the greatest ease of use through decades of time with minimal maintenance.

Historic windows are designed to operate smoothly with greater tolerances to building movement and other issues that inevitably arise. Spring tensioned or other mechanical parts made from thin pieces of plastic or metal cause replacement windows to become harder and harder to operate after years of use and require full scale replacement once broken.

5. Old windows pose a lead hazard

It's likely that your old windows have lead paint, but through the restoration process, nearly all of the lead paint is removed, resulting in a safe and lead free window.

Lead paint is not the hazard the media makes it out to be. Yes, children eating paint chips is a dangerous thing, but having lead paint safely encapsulated behind decades of other paint does not create a hazard. Read more about lead paint safety on The Craftsman Blog.

6. Restoration and maintenance of historic windows is more expensive than replacement

Every project should be looked at with an eye toward the Return on Investment (ROI) of the work. Replacement windows have an average ROI of 41.5 years Source: California State Parks Office of Historic Preservation. And since the typical life span of replacement windows is only 15-25 years, that makes replacement windows a very bad investment, despite the exaggerated claims from windows companies about how much you'll save with their products.

The truth is that the "no maintenance" claims of replacement windows equates to the fact that their windows are not able to be maintained. Regular maintenance of historic windows can be done by a homeowner (or professional if there isn't time in your schedule.)

If you keep up with the minimal maintenance on an annual basis, then you're looking at 5 minutes and $2 per window maximum to prevent small problems from becoming big ones, extending their life into centuries of use instead of just a couple of decades. That's how old windows save you money over the long haul!

CHAPTER 1
WINDOW BASICS

How to Use This Guide

My purpose in writing this book is to show you that anyone can restore wood windows themselves. And my promise is to give you the simplest (and fastest) process without all of the unnecessary clutter of other window books.

This is a practical, no-frills guide to get your wood windows from rotten, stuck in place, eye sores to beautiful, operable, historic pieces of your old home.

You don't need large machines and a full woodworking shop. You don't need heirloom hand planes and carving tools. All you need is a work table and some basic hand tools. Sure, there are tools that can make the process a little easier and faster, but window restoration as done by the pros is still done by hand, much the way I've laid out in this book.

In this guide, I've boiled down the dozens of books on the subject of window restoration that I've read and turned them into a simple and tested process that anyone with even the most rudimentary DIY skills can accomplish.

In part 1 there are things that we won't get to cover, and that doesn't mean they aren't important, but I believe they aren't necessary for most double-hung window restorations. If 9 out of 10 windows work one way, I'll focus on that one way rather than getting lost in the minutiae. In part 2 we'll get into some of those more specific items.

Small Victories

Part 1 will walk you through the basic phases of restoration necessary for wood windows and their components. You don't have to do everything in one weekend, though it is more efficient to do the work in larger chunks to avoid multiple setup and cleanup sessions.

I've broken the work down into the different sections so that you can work at your own pace. Maybe you get the mechanics working one weekend and then get ready to restore the jambs the second, and work on the sash on the third weekend.

The point is that you can make this work with your schedule so that it is an enjoyable process and not full of stress. Also, don't take on the biggest, most difficult repairs first. Get your feet wet on the easier stuff first and build your confidence. Small victories can do wonders to help keep you motivated and moving forward. Break the work into doable portions and you'll enjoy it much more. After all, the best way to eat an elephant is one bite at a time.

Wood, Putty & Glass

Historic wood windows are simple things. Whenever I start feeling frustrated by a repair that I can't fix, I try to say to myself, "wood, putty & glass…wood, putty & glass…" That's all they are. Three simple, understandable ingredients that make up a window.

Today, simple things are often looked upon as inferior. We add this new feature and tweak that design, but there are some times when an item's simplicity is what makes it work so beautifully. That is the case with historic windows.

The replacement window industry would beg to differ. They'll tell you why you need extruded aluminum, triple-pane, argon filled, low-e coated windows and they will be quite convincing about it.

They are out there to sell you a product and to sell it often. There is a joke in my profession that says they are called "replacement windows" because you have to continually replace them. The truth isn't far off.

Once you start down the road of replacement windows, you will ultimately need more replacement windows as these inferior products wear out quickly. Replacement windows are built with planned obsolescence in their design. They are made to slowly wear out and then be replaced by a newer "better" model next year.

Just like how the car companies change the styles of their cars to make your older model seem out of date, replacement window makers are constantly touting the next best thing- telling you that last year's model is woefully out of date and a total energy hog compared to this year's new and improved model.

Now, let's compare that to your original wood windows that were designed with longevity in mind. Original wood windows were built with resilient, old-growth wood and beautiful craftsmanship. Unlike replacement windows, historic wood windows were made to be easily repaired when issues arise and don't need wholesale replacement due to a failed component.

Historic wood windows, whether they are double-hung, casement or fixed, can last almost indefinitely when cared for properly. Until the 1950s, these were the most popular type of windows in homes across America and had been for hundreds of years.

Window Anatomy

The easiest way to understand how your old window works is to break it down into its parts and see how they all fit together. Once you understand where everything goes and what it does, you'll have an easier time in the restoration process.

At the end of this chapter there is a diagram of a traditional wood window. It's in an easy to find spot in the book, but go ahead and book mark it and use it as a reference whenever you need. Below I have listed all of the parts and their purpose. Come back to this page as a reference as well at any time during the process.

- **Access Door** - Small door cut into side of jamb to allow access to sash weights without removing casings.
- **Apron** - Lowest piece of interior casing just below the stool.
- **Blind Stop** - Exterior most guide to keep the upper sash in proper alignment.
- **Casing** - Interior decorative trim around window to help blend in transition from jamb to plaster walls.
- **Interior Stop** - Removable interior molding that holds the bottom sash in its proper position.
- **Jamb** - The frame that is installed into the rough opening in the walls and hold the sash in proper position.
- **Lift** - Placed on bottom rail to enable easier opening and closing of bottom sash.
- **Lock/Latch** - Securely locks window at meeting rail to prevent drafts and provide security.
- **Meeting Rail** - The beveled rail on both sash where they meet when in the closed position.
- **Muntin** - The small piece of wood that divides individual panes of glass within a sash.
- **Parting Bead/Strip** - Removable strip of wood that divides or "parts" the upper sash from the lower sash located in the middle of the jamb.
- **Pulley** - Mechanism for sash cord and weight to travel on enabling smooth up and down movement of sash.
- **Putty** - Seals individual panes of glass against weather.
- **Rail** - A horizontal wood member of the sash.
- **Sash** - The moveable parts of the window. There is an upper sash and lower sash and both can move independently on double-hung windows.
- **Sash Chain** - A strong and decorative option to attach the sash to the weights.

- **Sash Cord** - Braided cotton rope designed to attach the sash to the weights.
- **Sash Weight** - Cast iron or lead counterweight hidden behind casings to hold sash in proper position.
- **Sill** - Sloped exterior portion of the jamb that the bottom sash rests upon when closed.
- **Sill Horn/Nosing** - Exterior trim component installed just below sill to aid in shedding of water.
- **Stile** - A vertical wood member of the sash.
- **Stool** - Interior horizontal piece of casing that the bottom sash closes against.

Take a bit of time to familiarize yourself with these components on your own windows. There are lots of variations on sizes and styles of windows, but these components are all there in one form or another. Once you can identify these parts on your window, you're ready to get started!

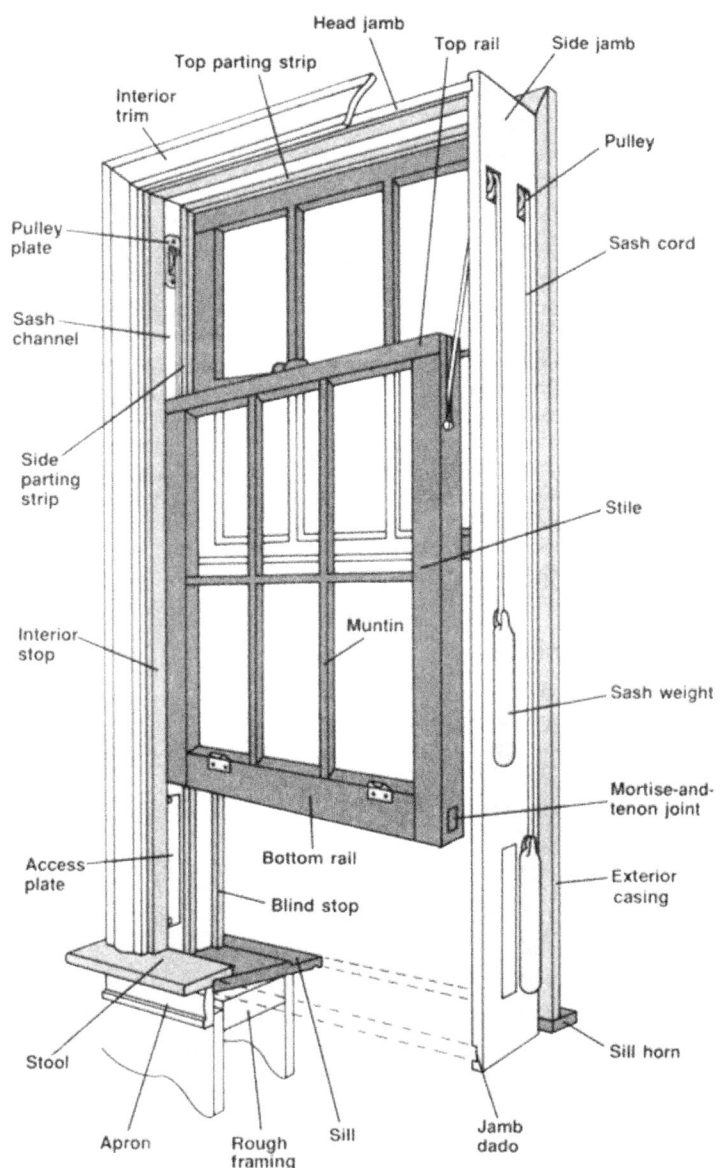

Old Windows In-Depth

CHAPTER 2
SAFETY FIRST

Any time you are scraping, sanding, or disturbing any surface in an old home, you need to be aware of the possible health risks associated and how to ensure that you and your family are protected. Wood windows are often home to two specific threats you need to be extra careful of.

LEAD PAINT

Any paint from before 1978 has a good chance of containing lead, especially on and around windows. If you are working on historic wood windows, you are well-advised to use lead safe work practices.

I'll talk about some lead safe work practices here, but for a comprehensive understanding of how to work safely with lead paint, you should visit the EPA's lead safe website at www2.epa.gov/lead.

If in doubt, assume your windows have lead paint and treat them accordingly, especially if you have little children around. Lead paint is extremely toxic to children under 6 years old, but with lead safe work practices, you can protect your family.

ASBESTOS

Wood and steel windows glazed from the 1920s-1950s occasionally contain asbestos in the glazing putty and caulk. Just like lead paint, asbestos is not something to scoff at. Before you plan to do any work on your windows, I would advise you to test the glazing putty for asbestos.

Asbestos testing is not something that can be done yourself. You'll have to chip out a small amount of putty, place it in a bag, and take it to a local testing facility or mail it to a company like Western Analytics at www.asbestostesting.com. The charge for testing is usually between $20-40.

Whether it is lead paint or asbestos, you as the homeowner, are allowed to do the work yourself. So, if you decide to move forward with the restoration of your wood windows and they have both of these threats, protect yourself with the proper respirator and try to work dust free in your restoration. I'll talk about the best ways to minimize dust in the next section.

Lead Safe Work Practices

The EPA calls these techniques "lead safe work practices" and they are just that. If you follow these instructions, you can ensure that everyone in the house (whether they are doing the work or not) will be safe from exposure to unsafe levels of lead.

There are 3 keys to working safely with lead paint:
- Proper Setup & Cleanup
- PPE (Personal Protective Equipment)
- Low-Dust Work Techniques

Setup & Cleanup

Working Outdoors

Outdoor containment isn't nearly as difficult, so we'll talk about that first. The goal here is to keep lead paint from getting into the dirt and plantings around the house that little children might be tempted to play in. You want to be able to wrap everything up and not be picking pieces of old paint out of the dirt for the rest of the day.

> **PRO TIP**
>
> Staple the plastic to a 2x4 and lay that right up against the building. This will keep the plastic from bunching up or leaving gaps right next to the building. This is where the most debris will fall, so you want it covered well.

Setup
- Choose a relatively calm day with low wind to do exterior work.
- Lay down 6 mil plastic within a 10 foot perimeter of the area you are working.
- For extra safety, place some stakes and caution tape or signage to mark off the work area and keep passersby from entering it.

Cleanup
- Vacuum up any remaining debris with a HEPA vac.

- Mist the plastic with water and roll up the plastic (keeping the small debris like paint chips inside of it) and place it in a contractor bag or other thick walled plastic trash bag. Roll the neck of the bag into a gooseneck and tape it shut.
- Using a HEPA vacuum, clean off work surfaces and wipe them down with TSP to make sure they are free of any remaining dust.
- Dispose of the bag with normal trash. It does not need to be disposed of as hazardous waste, contrary to what a lot of people think.

Working Indoors

This is where things are more complicated and you need to be more vigilant about your containment and cleanup. The interior of your home will need to pass the "white glove" test when you're done working to ensure all is safe.

Please be careful to follow these guidelines.

Create a sealed off workspace with plastic

Setup

- Remove any furniture within 6 feet of your proposed work area.
- Tape down 6 mil. plastic in a 6′ perimeter around your work area to protect the floor.
- Create the bubble: You can use painter's tape and plastic from floor to ceiling, but I prefer using a zip wall system to quickly stretch plastic from floor to ceiling. It's much easier, and unlike tape, which can start falling down, the zip wall holds everything tight. You can also get zippers that attach to the plastic to create an easy access door in and out of the work area. Trust me on this, it's worth the extra expense if you are doing more than one day's worth of work.
- Plastic or completely tape over any HVAC vents or returns within the enclosed area and turn off the HVAC system while you are working. This may seem like overkill, but you don't want to be circulating lead dust around the house.
- Tape over any electrical outlets as well since dust can settle into those little crevices. It will make cleanup much easier.

Old Windows In-Depth

- Set a damp towel on the floor just outside the entrance to the work area. This will prevent you from tracking any dust or debris out of the work area as you need to come and go.

Cleanup
- Clean your way out of the work area. Start at the corner or wall and work your way out of the room.
- Once you've finished with all the work, mist down all the plastic, roll it up dirty side in and place it in a contractor bag or other thick walled plastic trash bag. Roll the neck of the bag into a gooseneck and tape it shut.
- Using a HEPA vacuum, clean up ALL of the surfaces (walls, floors, trim, etc.)
- Wipe down ALL of the surfaces with a rag moistened with TSP. You may have to do this a couple of times until the rag comes out clean. *Remember the white glove test.*

PPE (Personal Protective Equipment)

Lead safe work practices are not just about protecting the other people living in the house. You need to protect yourself since you'll be front and center making dust and tearing things apart.

There are lots of options to keep you safe and a lot of it is personal preference, but I'll give you the basics that you need to address before starting any project.

- ***Goggles or safety glasses*** - These aren't specific to lead hazards, but you should protect your most vulnerable and important feature when doing any work.
- ***Respirator*** - A standard dust mask won't cut it. You'll need at minimum a P100 or N100 respirator. They make disposable masks that you can get for about $10 on Amazon.
- ***Coveralls*** - A full body suit isn't necessary if you aren't doing this as a career, but it can still be helpful to keep your clothes free of lead dust. If you don't wear a suit, then be sure that you wash any contaminated clothing separately and keep it away from any children or pregnant women.
- ***Shower*** – What's the first thing you do when you're done working? Take a shower and wash off thoroughly. You want any traces of lead safely washed down the drain before you do anything else.

Low-Dust Work Techniques

Last but not least, you need to work safely. Some techniques create way too much dust. Others can vaporize lead, rendering your respirator worthless. Moral of the story…work safe. Here are some major Do's and Don'ts when working with lead paint.

Don't
- Use grinders, power sanders, planers, sand blasting or other abrasive power tools without a HEPA vac attachment.
- Use high-heat paint removal (torches, heat guns, electric heat plates, etc.)
- Wet surfaces when using power tools due to the risk of electrical shock.

Do
- Use HEPA vac attachments and dust collection shrouds with any power tools.
- Use low-heat infrared paint removers (Speedheater, Silent Paint Remover or similar)
- Use chemical paint strippers.
- Wet surfaces prior to using pneumatic tools or hand scraping to help control dust.
- Use steam heat for paint removal.

I do want to clarify a couple of things about using heat for paint removal. Low temperatures can be safe for lead paint removal. Anything below about 1,000° F is generally considered safe for lead paint removal. Temperatures above that point can cause the lead to vaporize, which creates an enormous health hazard.

Not to mention that using high temperature paint removal techniques can also lead to house fires. Not just in the moment, but sometimes hours later smoldering building components can finally burst into flames. In my opinion, high heat means high danger!

So, that's it. You've got the basics of working safely with lead paint. Just remember that this isn't just about paint removal. You should be doing lead safe work practices anytime you renovate a house that tests positive for lead paint.

Chapter 3
Mechanical Restoration

The first step in restoring your windows is to get them moving again. We'll break them free of decades of paint and caulk and change out the ropes here. There is nothing pretty about this part of the work, but without getting your sash moving, we won't be able to do any other work on the window.

Windows can be restored in place to an extent, but there are some elements that can't be worked on unless the sash are removed from the jambs. Sash were designed to be removed for repair or cleaning, and though they may be stubbornly in place today, you can remove them without doing damage to the sash or the jamb.

Materials List

- Roll of 3-6 mil. Plastic Sheeting
- Contractor Bags
- Trisodium Phosphate Cleaner (TSP)
- Respirator (N100 or P100)
- Safety Glasses
- Masking/Painter's Tape
- WD-40 or DryLube Spray
- Parting Bead Stock
- 60-grit sandpaper
- Sanding Block

Tool List

- Trim Pry-bar
- Hammer
- Firm Putty Knife
- HEPA Vacuum
- Nail Puller/Nipper
- Screwdriver
- Duck Bill Vise-Grips
- Razor Knife
- Window Zipper

STEP 1
Prep

Alright, you've got all your tools and materials in hand and you're ready to start! Take a look at the windows you plan to work on and figure out the best way to get access to them. Are they 1st or 2nd story? Covered by thorny bushes? Maybe they are easy to access like the picture on the next page.

Whatever the scenario, make a plan for how you will proceed with the work before you get into things and realize there was a better or safer way to do it. Start with the steps below.

Action Steps

1. Test for the presence of lead paint.
2. Choose a calm day with good weather for your exterior work.
3. Remove any obstructions and prepare the work area using the lead safe work practices covered earlier.
4. Wear safety glasses and P100 lead rated respirator at all times during work.
5. Wash hands thoroughly with soap before eating or drinking anything on the job site. In general, do not eat or drink anywhere near the work to prevent ingesting any lead paint.

STEP 2
REMOVE INTERIOR STOP

The first thing you need to do is get the sash out of the jamb. Depending on how much built up paint and caulk there is, this may be simple or difficult. Get both the bottom and top sash out before moving onto anything else.

The first piece to remove is the stop. This is a small piece of trim that is usually nailed in place along the side of the jamb. Some stops are screwed in place, which will have to be unscrewed and then gently pried off. You want to avoid breaking the stops, though if they do break, they can be replaced with stock moldings available to most lumber yards or home stores.

The window stop was designed to be removed to service the window, so don't worry that you are doing something wrong by prying this piece off. What makes it difficult is usually decades of excess paint or unnecessary extra nails by an overzealous handyman.

To get your sash out, you only need to remove the stop on one side, but you can remove both if you want to clean them up more thoroughly.

Action Steps

1. Gently score the paint between the stop and the jamb and the stool and the sash with a razor knife, being careful not to gouge the wood. Don't cut too deeply, just enough to cut through the paint bond.
2. Using a trim pry bar or firm putty knife, gently pry the stop away from the jamb. Some stops will be installed using screws and washers instead of finish nails. These must be unscrewed.
3. Remove any remaining nails from the stop with a nail puller by pulling them through the back side of the stop.
4. Scrape the backside of the stop that runs against the sash with a carbide scraper to clean away any built up paint or caulk.
5. Number the back of the stop to go with the corresponding window and set aside for reinstallation later.
6. Pull any remaining nails that may be left in the jamb.

> **PRO TIP**
>
> Stops come in all different shapes and sizes, but it will always be in the same location, and that is the tip to identifying it correctly.

1. Score paint line on interior stop

2. Pry stop away from jamb

STEP 3
REMOVE BOTTOM SASH

The bottom sash is the most inside sash, and so it must be removed first before you can gain access to the top sash. The bottom sash is usually much easier to remove than the top sash, so it's the place to start.

While you can cut the paint free on the exterior, it's usually easiest to simply focus on the interior when it comes to the bottom sash and let the majority of the exterior paint buildup break off as you remove the sash.

If your bottom sash is not painted shut, then that eliminates all this cutting of paint and caulk and it is that much easier to remove.

Action Steps

1. Cut the paint seal between the bottom sash and the remaining stop and possibly between the bottom sash and stool if necessary.
2. Insert a firm putty knife in between the meeting rails and gently pry the sash loose to break the paint seal. Lift the sash above the stool to remove it.
3. Swing the side of the lower sash where the interior stop was removed inward to access the rope mortise on the side of the sash.
4. Remove the knotted rope from the rope mortise being careful not to let the sash drop or the rope (which is attached to the hidden weights) fly out of your grasp. Sometimes the rope may be nailed into the side of the sash. This nail will require removal in order to get the knot out.
5. Gently allow the rope knot to rest against the pulley. If the knot isn't big enough to keep the rope from falling back into the pocket, tie a larger knot.
6. Repeat the process on the other side of the bottom sash.
7. If you are doing multiple windows, number the sash on the side so that it can be reinstalled into the proper window later.
8. Scrape, slice, or sand away unnecessary paint buildup on sash that may prevent movement.

2. Pry sash apart at meeting rail

3. Swing sash inward to reveal rope mortise

Old Windows In-Depth

STEP 4
REMOVE PARTING BEAD

Steps 4 and 5 are pretty much done at the same time because the easiest way to remove the parting bead is to have the top sash lowered all the way to the sill. So, that means cutting it free of paint and caulk.

The parting bead may be painted and caulked so much so that it looks like it should not be removed, but it is a separate piece that was designed to be removed in order to remove the top sash.

Parting bead can be eternally frustrating, but duck-billed vise grips are its nemesis. Some parting bead will be nailed in place, and others will be simply pressure fit. Either way requires the parting bead to be pulled straight out of the channel it rests in and then removed (often in pieces).

Action Steps

1. Cut parting bead free of paint or caulk at top sash using a razor knife or window zipper.
2. Work the sash up and down until you can lower it all the way down to the sill.
3. Starting at the top and working your way down, use duck billed vise grips to grasp the parting bead and wiggle it back and forth to work it loose.
4. Cut and fit new parting beads if necessary.
5. Scrape excess paint from existing parting beads.
6. Prep parting beads for paint and reinstallation.

> **PRO TIP**
>
> Parting beads often break when removing them. It is a good idea to have extras on hand, or extra wood to make new ones if necessary.

1. Cut parting bead free of top sash

3. Using duck-bill vise-grips remove parting bead

STEP 5
REMOVE TOP SASH

Ah, the top sash. Most people don't believe that this part of the window ever moved, but on double-hung windows, they are most definitely mistaken. There are single-hung windows where the top sash is stationary and will not move, so before you get too deeply into this work, make sure that your windows are not single-hung.

Top sashes are usually so gummed up that they are almost impossible to move without major effort. When cut free of paint, the top sash will move all the way down to the sill, but getting it there is a challenge. If you have serious paint building up and the sash barely budges, keep working it up and down to try to gain as much motion as possible.

If the top sash absolutely won't go down to the sill, it can still come out as long as you can have it lowered enough to reveal the pulleys. If the pulley is revealed and your parting bead is out, go ahead and try to swing the side out and remove the sash from the jamb.

Action Steps

1. Cut all paint seals around top sash with a razor knife or window zipper. The window zipper is good because it has little files that sand away the paint buildup in the paint joint once the paint seal is broken.
2. Move the top sash all the way down to the window sill. If the sash will not move due to paint build up, you can continue, but the parting bead will be more difficult to remove and will likely come out in pieces.
3. After the parting bead is out of one side, swing that side of the sash inward and remove the ropes as with the bottom sash.
4. Be sure to number the sash.
5. Scrape, slice or sand away unnecessary paint buildup on blind stop and jamb that may prevent smooth movement of the sash.

> **PRO TIP**
>
> Occasionally there is a screw, nail or block of wood someone has installed to keep the top sash from coming down. Make sure to check and remove this if present.

1. Score paint line on blind spot exterior

3. Swing one side inward to remove rope

Old Windows In-Depth

35

STEP 6
ROPE REMOVAL

Rope removal is pretty straight forward if your house has weight pocket access doors. Not every house does. Some builders were cheap and didn't add this feature, which makes changing ropes much more difficult.

If you are missing access doors then you are left with 2 options. 1) Cut your own access doors 2) Remove the interior casings so that you can get to the weights. Neither is particularly fun, but they both work.

If you have access doors, then you'll have to remove the retaining screw and pry the door open. This door was usually cut in place and sometimes wasn't even cut all the way through, which can make it difficult to pry out. I find that a firm putty knife fits nicely and allows me to get the door open.

Also, try to remember which door goes where. They were each cut by hand and will only fit in the place they came from.

Action Steps

1. Open the weight pocket access doors on either side of jamb by removing retaining screws and prying the door open.
2. Cut the knot so that the remaining rope can slide back through pulley and the weight can be removed. If you don't plan to remove the pulleys for restoration, skip to Step 7. If you plan to remove the pulleys then remove the weights and mark them as to which sash (upper or lower) they belong to. Upper sash are sometimes heavier and require heavier weights. If your weights are all the same weight, there is no need to mark them.

> **PRO TIP**
>
> Ensure there is a bottom ledge inside of your weight pockets before cutting ropes. Sometimes weights can fall irretrievably deep into the wall when the rope is cut.

Old Windows In-Depth

1. Remove screw from access door

2. Remove old rope from weights

Old Windows In-Depth

37

STEP 7
ROPE INSTALLATION

My recommended sash rope for the majority of wood windows is Samson Spot Cord #8, though there are locally available options at hardware stores. The important thing is for the rope to be braided cotton and NOT fully synthetic rope, because they can stretch over time.

For very heavy (50+ lbs.) sash, you can install chains, but for the majority of windows, rope is the best option due to its affordability, availability and durability. Good sash rope can last 60+ years.

Action Steps

1. Measure the entire height of the jamb and cut new ropes to that length.
2. Tie a single knot in one end of the rope.
3. Feed the untied end of the rope through the top of the pulley until the bottom of the rope is reachable through the weight pocket access door.
4. Attach the rope to the weight with a bow knot displayed on the following page. When tying off your weights, make sure that the weight is floating just above the sill when the rope knot is resting against the face of the pulley. If the weight bottoms out on the sill, then it will not be supporting the weight of the sash.
5. Lubricate pulleys with WD-40 or DryLube spray if necessary.
6. Place the weights back into the weight pocket and test operation along the entire length the rope must travel by pulling the knot from the pulley.
7. If operation is smooth, reinstall access door with original screws, making sure door is completely flush with jamb.

> **PRO TIP**
>
> If your rope won't feed all the way down the pocket, try taping a screw or fishing weight to the end to help it make its way down to the bottom of the pocket.

3. Feed rope into pulley

4. Tie off weights with a bow knot

STEP 8
Finishing Up

You've now restored the mechanical aspects of your windows. Way to go! Now what? Well, that depends on how ambitious you are. If you are ready to tackle the jamb restoration, now is the best time to do it while you have the sash out and everything is ready.

If you are ready to call it a day, you can either reinstall the sash or board everything up with plywood until you're ready for the next step. If you are finished for the day, remember to clean everything up being sure to follow the lead-safe work practices that I outlined earlier.

When you're ready, we can move on to the next chapter and learn to restore the jambs. Realize that so far, you've done more to a double-hung window than most people even knew was possible. You now know how it functions, and even if you aren't restoring all of your windows, you can take care of simple tasks like changing a broken rope with confidence.

Knowledge is power and you've got some power now. So, when you're ready, let's get some more knowledge about these jambs and how to bring them back to life!

Chapter 4
Jamb Restoration

The jamb is the frame that the sash rest in. The jamb will not be removed from the opening, but should be restored in place.

There are two big issues when restoring the jamb. The first is paint build up. This is usually the culprit for sash that are stuck in place. Removing this paint down to bare wood without gouging the wood can be a lot of work, but this will give you the best results and smoothest operation when you reinstall your windows.

The second issue is rot/termite damage. There may be no damage or extensive damage, depending on any number of factors. If the damage is serious, it may include full scale replacement of the jamb. Usually this is not the case, but be prepared for the possibility.

Once the jambs are restored, board them up with plywood or plexiglass until the sash are restored and ready to be reinstalled. If you're lucky enough to live in a house where exterior storms are installed, you can use those as temporary enclosures while the sash are out for repair.

Materials List

- Roll of 3-6 mil. Plastic Sheeting
- TSP Cleaner
- Respirator (N100 or P100)
- Safety Glasses
- Nitrile Gloves
- Masking/Painter's Tape
- Mineral Spirits
- Exterior Oil-based Primer
- 1 1/4" Screws
- 1/2" Plywood
- WoodEpox & LiquidWood
- Acetone
- Enamel Finish Paint

Tool List

- HEPA Vacuum
- Pull Scraper (ProScraper vacuum scraper recommended)
- Awl/Chisel
- Screwdriver
- Drill/Driver
- Razor Knife
- Disposable Chip Brushes
- Paint Brush

STEP 1
JAMB PAINT REMOVAL

Clean jambs are essential to smooth operation of your windows. Likely, you have decades of paint built up, which has been causing the sash to stick in their jambs and not operate. Removing this build up down to bare wood will free up your windows and also serves to reveal any damaged wood that may be hiding behind the paint.

You don't have to remove every bit of paint, but you want the bulk of the build up removed. While you can use chemical paint strippers or infrared heat for this, I believe that using a quality carbide pull scraper is the best way to go. It's clean, fume free, and a good workout too.

Focus on removing paint from the areas between the stop and the blind stop. This is the area that needs to be clean in order for the sash to move freely and smoothly. All the other areas are merely cosmetic.

Before I start scraping, I remove all of the remaining parting bead to allow the larger 2" blade on our ProScrapers to fit. You don't have to remove it all, but you'll need a scraper that is no wider than 1 1/4" in order to fit in the sash tracks if the parting bead remains and that can slow things down.

Action Steps

1. Remove all of the remaining parting bead. This allows easier access for scraping of the jambs.
2. Being careful not to gouge the wood, scrape all paint and other residue from the inside of the blind stop to the inside of the interior stop including all the jambs and the sill to bare wood using a pull style carbide scraper. I recommend the ProScraper, which is a carbide tipped hollow body scraper that can be attached to a HEPA vacuum to eliminate airborne dust and debris.
3. Wipe surfaces down with a rag moistened with TSP.

> **PRO TIP**
>
> Always scrape in the direction of the grain to avoid tearing out chunks of wood. Wood grain always runs along the length of the board not the width.

2. Scrape jambs free of paint

Tip: Be sure to scrape behind blind stop and in corners

STEP 2
Jamb Wood Repair

Most repairs on rotted jambs can be completed using this epoxy system, although some jambs may have more extensive damage and require replacement parts to be milled by an experienced carpenter.

A word of caution about working with these epoxies: I have seen many a time when an epoxy repair done by a novice has created a bigger mess than they started with. Start small and start simple. Don't try massive reconstruction of things until you have a feel and understanding for how this epoxy works. It is always easier to apply a little epoxy and then go back and add more later than to glob it on and create a problem for yourself. If the damage is too severe, don't be afraid to call in a pro.

Action Steps

1. Dig out loose/damaged wood with an awl or chisel and vacuum out debris.
2. Make sure the wood is dry and there is not rain expected.
3. Keep acetone handy for clean up.
4. In a disposable container, mix parts A & B in equal amounts of LiquidWood. Wait 5-10 mins. and apply to areas requiring epoxy repair and rotted portions or wood with a disposable brush. It should be applied in the same amount and fashion as if you were painting the area. Wait 10-15 mins. for it to begin curing.
5. Mix parts A & B in equal amounts of WoodEpox until blended well and firmly press into damaged areas while LiquidWood is still slightly tacky. Make sure the repair sits a little proud of the surface so that you can sand it level later. Shape and smooth surface using a plastic putty knife. If the filler sticks to the knife, you can wipe a little LiquidWood or acetone on the knife to help it glide more easily. Don't make a big mound here or you will pay for it later by sanding and chiseling away epoxy for hours.
6. Once the epoxy has cured and hardened (as little as one hour for large repairs and overnight for small repairs and during cold weather) using a chisel or scraper, level out the surface and sand smooth using 80-120 grit sandpaper.

> **PRO TIP**
>
> Most epoxies won't cure below 50°F and can cure extremely quickly in high heat. Larger repairs also cure quicker than small ones. So, plan accordingly.

4. Apply LiquidWood to damaged areas

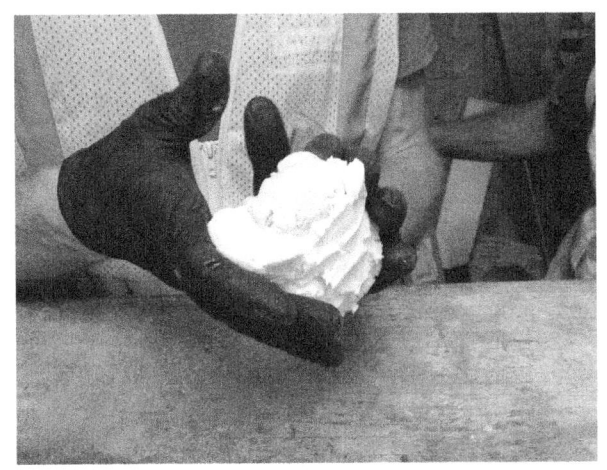

5. Mix equal parts WoodEpox until uniform in color

5. Firmly press into damaged areas

5. Smooth with a disposable putty knife

Old Windows In-Depth

STEP 3
JAMB PRIMING & PAINTING

Many window jambs were not painted originally due to the fact that painting these surfaces almost inevitably leads to sticking windows. If your jambs were originally bare and you decide not to prime or paint, then that is just fine.

If you do decide to paint, use an oil-based paint or a quality water-based enamel that does not remain tacky after it has dried. Using a regular house paint in the jambs will result in windows that constantly stick and may not even move in hot, humid weather.

While painting, you don't have to paint in the channel that the parting bead will eventually go into. In fact, it's better to not paint there, which could make fitting your parting bead difficult due to a gummed up channel later.

Action Steps

1. Once the paint removal is finished and your repairs have been completed, vacuum up any remaining debris and wipe the jambs and surrounding areas down using a cotton rag and TSP cleaner.
2. Apply a coat of exterior grade oil-based primer to the jambs and sill.
3. Once the primer has dried, sand it lightly with a fine sanding sponge.
4. Apply two thin coats of finish paint to the jambs and sill in your preferred color.

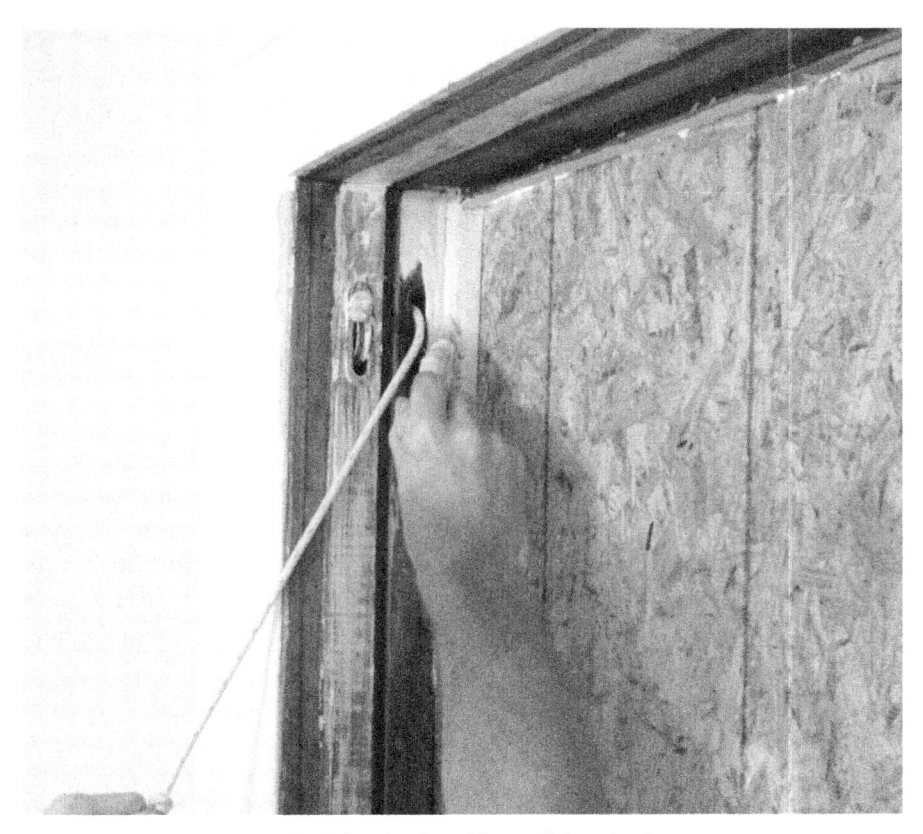

2. Prime jambs with an oil-based primer

STEP 4
PARTING BEAD & STOP

If you are keeping the original parting bead and stop, they should be scraped clean of any remaining paint and primed and painted just like the jambs.

If you are replacing either, then new stock should be purchased or milled and primed and painted prior to reinstalling the finished sash. Parting bead is available at most lumber yards in the molding department. If not, you can make your own on a table saw. The common size is 3/4" x 1/2", but be sure to check what size your parting bead is before you mill a ton of it.

Keep in mind that if you add a coat of primer to the parting bead and 2 coats of paint, it will not be the same thickness it was when you milled it and may not fit in the channel. Test your fit first and make adjustments before doing large batches.

Action Steps

1. Cut parting bead to length with a hand saw and make sure the bottom is cut at a 8°-10° bevel to match the sill angle.
2. Fit the top parting bead first and then each side by pressing it into place. Use a hammer and scrap piece of wood to bang it into place if the fit is tight. Leave one side out, which will be installed later with the top sash.

> **PRO TIP**
>
> Make the parting bead just slightly smaller than you think, otherwise you'll spend all day trying to force it into an opening too small for the bead.

1. Beveled bottom of parting bead

2. Primed jambs with parting bead awaiting restored sash

STEP 5
COVER OPENINGS

Sash restoration usually takes at least a week due to drying times of putty and paint, so you'll need to protect the gaping hole left by the removal of the sash. If you have exterior storm windows, then you're already protected. If not, then 1/2" plywood or OSB works great for this temporary protection. Some people prefer plexiglass to let the light in, and you can use this if you don't mind the extra expense.

The best option is to use two pieces of plywood and screw them in from the interior. When you cut your plywood, make sure the top piece overlaps the bottom by a couple inches to prevent water from coming inside.

You can also install one big piece of plywood against the outside of the blind stop if you have easier access from the outside. If you do this, then I would use square or star drive screws or even a combination of bit types for added security. You don't want anyone with a screwdriver getting into your house.

Action Steps
1. Cut two overlapping pieces of plywood and install them against the inside of the blind stop. Make sure the top piece is installed first and it overlaps the exterior of the bottom piece to avoid water coming in.
2. Screw at an angle into the blind stop using 1 1/4" screws.

Two-piece plywood installed from the inside (top first then bottom)

One-piece plywood installed from the outside

CHAPTER 5
HARDWARE RESTORATION

Old hardware is some of the most beautiful, character filled elements of your old windows once restored.

Often, after years of paint build up and rust, the hardware ceases to function smoothly, if at all. Locks, lifts, and pulleys come in a variety of styles and sizes, and the restoration process is much the same no matter what type of hardware you have.

The focus here is paint and rust removal. Once they are cleaned up, the hardware usually functions like new. Some may need more work to get the mechanics working again, though.

If a piece of hardware is too far gone, then a suitable replacement can usually be found at an architectural salvage yard or from online replacement hardware companies like House of Antique Hardware, VanDyke's Restorers, Strybuc or Robert Brooke & Associates.

MATERIALS LIST

- Respirator (N100 or P100)
- Safety Glasses
- Disposable Cotton Rags
- Satin Spray Lacquer
- #8 1" Brass Screws
- #6 1" Brass Screws
- Steel Wool (000 & 0000)
- Dish Soap or Baking Soda
- WD-40 or DryLube Spray

TOOL LIST

- Screwdriver (flat & Phillips)
- Hammer
- Razor Knife
- Crock Pot
- Nail Nippers
- Bench Grinder w/ Wire Wheel (optional)

STEP 1
PULLEY RESTORATION

If your pulleys don't move smoothly, then your windows don't move smoothly. Do your best to get things cleaned up and moving. It may take a little trouble shooting and bending of parts before you get things back in order, but most hardware just needs a good cleaning to function like new.

Follow the steps below depending on what types of pulleys you have.

Action Steps

1. Press-fit Pulleys
   - Do not remove press-fit pulleys, as they will damage the jamb and possibly break during removal.
   - Clean press-fit pulleys of excess paint and rust using a dull chisel or steel wool.
   - Using flat pliers, bend any portions of the pulley wheel back into shape to allow smooth operation.
   - If the pulley is not functional, spray with a rust treatment like WD-40 and slowly work the functionality back into the pulley, wipe clean.

2. Screw-in Pulleys
   - Remove these pulleys from the jambs and clean the faces of rust and paint by cooking them in an old crock pot with water and soap for a couple of hours until the paint can be removed with a firm nylon bristle brush.
   - If the pulley is not functional, spray with a rust treatment like WD-40 and slowly work the functionality back into the pulley, wipe clean.
   - Wipe clean and apply 2 even coats of clear satin spray lacquer on ferrous metals. Bronze can be left bare to develop a natural patina.
   - Once dry, reinstall pulleys into painted jambs to prepare for rope/chain installation using #8 or #9 size 3/4" flat head brass wood screws or original screws.

Various types of window pulleys

STEP 2
Hardware Restoration

Remove any hardware from the sash prior to any sash restoration work and set it aside. Hardware usually needs built up paint removed and some buffing to remove rust, though sometimes it is more than cosmetic and may need replacement. Judge for yourself what your hardware needs and proceed accordingly.

Action Steps

1. Paint Removal - Place hardware in an old crock pot on high temp filled with water and a bit of dish soap or baking soda. After cooking for a few hours, remove one piece at a time with pliers and using a stiff bristle brush clean the paint off then set aside to cool.
2. If moving parts aren't so moveable, apply a little WD-40 and slowly work operability back.
3. Buff the surface aggressively with 000 or 0000 steel wool to desired cleanliness and patina. Wipe hardware with clean rag when done.
4. Apply 2 coats of clear satin spray lacquer to any ferrous metal to prevent rust.
5. Reinstall hardware after sash restoration is complete using #6 1" brass screws or original screws.

> **PRO TIP**
>
> Solid bronze hardware doesn't need to be lacquered unless you want to. Bronze doesn't rust and it will gain a nice patina over the years if left bare.

1. Remove paint with stiff bristle brush

The finished product

STEP 3
AGING HARDWARE

Something completely new to this book is this section on aging new hardware to help it match the old hardware on your windows. Bronze and steel hardware ages pretty gracefully, if you ask me. Other than really beat up stuff that has gotten rusted and mangled, I prefer to keep the old hardware if it can be restored like we just discussed.

Old hardware darkens over time from exposure and develops a nice patina, which can be difficult to match with new factory finished hardware that always scratches off. Well, I've developed a product called the Patinator that will age new hardware to match your old hardware naturally.

For this process to work, you'll need un-lacquered brass, bronze, or steel hardware or if you can't get any un-lacquered versions, you'll need to strip the finish off of the new hardware with a wire wheel or other abrasive method. Once you have it ready, here is the process to age your hardware to match the good old stuff.

Action Steps

1. Fill a small container with Patinator so that the hardware will be completely submerged
2. Place the un-lacquered hardware in the Patinator until the desired level of patina is reached (usually 10-25 seconds)
3. Remove and immediately submerge in water to stop the aging process
4. Wipe with a clean cotton cloth to remove excess residue
5. Install on your window.

> **PRO TIP**
>
> If you darken it too much, you can polish off the patina with a wire wheel or steel wool and start again until you reach the right level of patina.

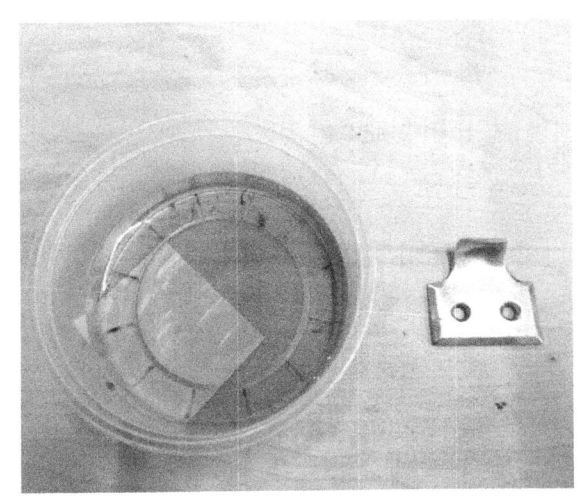

1. Fill bowl with Patinator

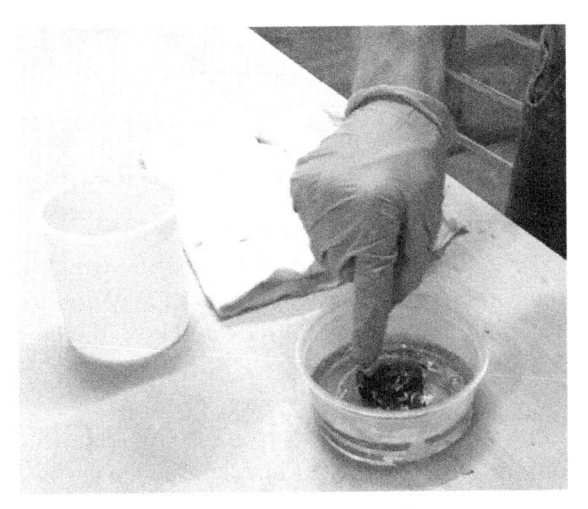

2. Soak in Patinator for 10-25 sec.

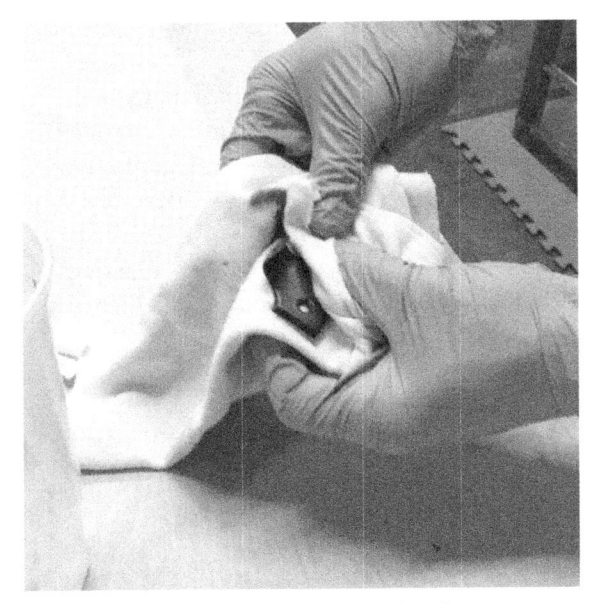

3 & 4. Dip in water and wipe clean

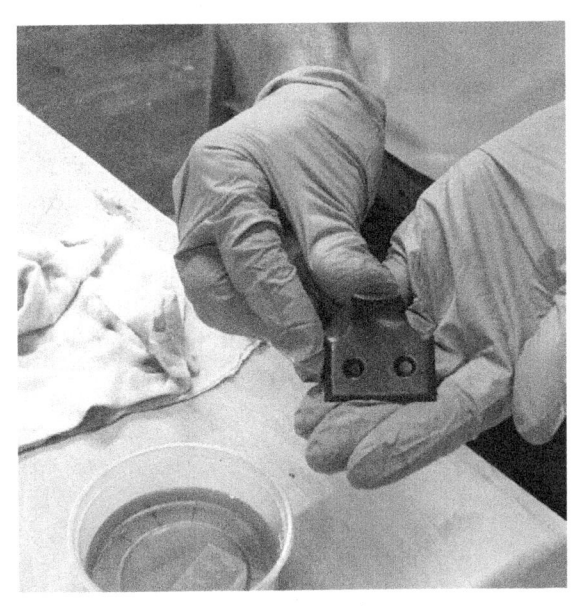

The finished product

Old Windows In-Depth

Chapter 6
Sash Restoration

The bulk of the work to restore wood windows has to do with sash restoration. Depending on the condition of your windows, you may not need to do a full restoration as detailed in this guide. Patching some worn out putty and keeping the paint touched up will do wonders to extend the life of a wood window.

If your windows have been severely neglected or you want to really make them sparkle, then a full restoration is the way to go. If you follow the process outlined below, your sash will look like they did the day they were originally installed and will last you another 100 years with minimal care.

This is your opportunity to really make these windows shine. A well restored sash is a total joy to see and handle. It slides smoothly in the jamb, the paint doesn't look chippy or worn, the profiles are clean from all the decades long build up of paint, and the glazing putty is smooth and crisp. This is where I like to spend the majority of my time in the restoration process.

So, let's get started. On the next page you'll find your list of tools and materials that you'll need for this phase. These are the basics, so feel free to upgrade as you wish and can afford. Better tools absolutely make the work go smoother and easier. Use sharp blades and fresh sandpaper often because the additional expense of them is minimal compared to the subpar and slow work results you will get from using dull or worn supplies.

One thing not mentioned is a good sturdy work table. If you plan on doing more than one window, it is worth it to build or purchase a worktable that can securely support your work. This phase involves a lot of hard work and working at the right height with a sash that is secure will make the process sooooo much easier and enjoyable.

MATERIALS LIST

- TSP Cleaner
- Respirator (N100 or P100)
- Safety Glasses
- Nitrile Gloves (optional)
- Disposable Cotton Rags
- Mineral Spirits
- Exterior Oil-based Primer
- WoodEpox & LiquidWood
- Glass Cleaner
- Glazing Putty
- Glazing Points
- Sandpaper (80 grit & 120-grit)
- Titebond III Wood Glue
- Enamel Finish Paint

TOOL LIST

- Hammer
- Firm Putty Knife
- HEPA Vacuum
- Pull Scraper (ProScraper recommended)
- Profile scrapers
- Screwdriver
- Clamps
- Razor Knife
- Disposable Chip Brushes
- Paint Brush

STEP 1
PAINT REMOVAL

The description may sound simple, but the work can be tedious here. Depending on the condition of the paint, this may be very easy or very difficult. It's not necessary to remove every trace of paint, but get the bulk of the paint off and ensure a smooth and level surface.

New paint is only as durable as the surface it is painted on, so, if you just paint right over peeling and cracking paint, then your new paint won't last long. So, the level of paint removal that is needed is really up to you and how long you want your new paint job to last, and how good you want it to look.

Take extra care when working on the interior profiles of the muntins as they can be easily gouged with scrapers or sanded into oblivion by a heavy hand. Be gentle and slow in these spots.

Work on a well supported table and you may find that clamping the sash to the table will help you work more efficiently.

Action Steps

1. Using a carbide scraper or preferably a ProScraper attached to a HEPA vacuum, scrape paint from all flat surfaces of the sash on both sides.
2. Using a combination of profile scrapers, razor knives or other tools, remove the paint from profiled surfaces on the muntins, being careful not to damage the delicate profiles. Work slowly and methodically here. It is very time consuming and slow work, but necessary all the same.

> **PRO TIP**
>
> On the interior of the muntins, just remove the loose and built up paint and then sand it smooth, or you'll spend all week just working on these little details.

1. Scrape flats with a pull scraper

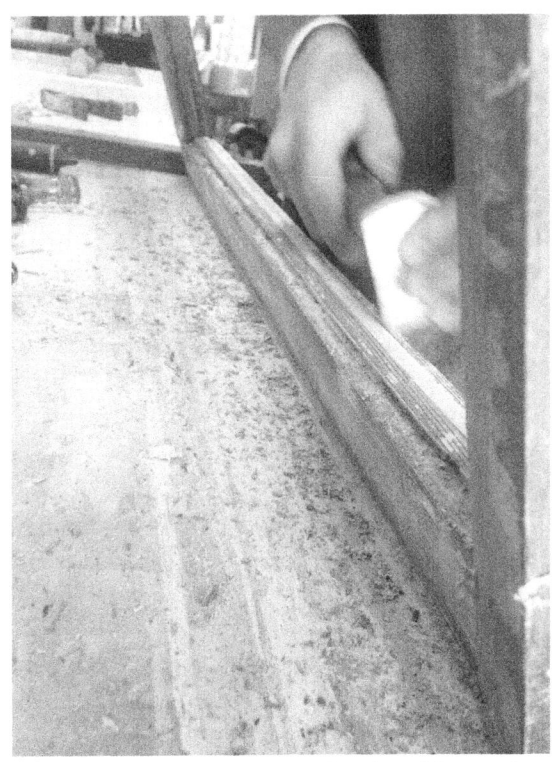

2. Carefully scrape interior profiles free of loose paint

STEP 2
DEGLAZING

Deglazing a sash refers to removing the glass. While it is not absolutely necessary to remove the glass in order to restore a sash, it makes for a far more thorough and lasting restoration.

You'll need to chip out all of the existing putty from the exterior of the sash. Use a chisel, putty knife, razor knife or any other tool that you find effective. Be careful through this process to not gouge the wood or break the glass. In part 2, I'll discuss using steam to deglaze windows which can work great to soften up the putty and make it much easier to not break glass.

The other thing to look out for are the tiny metal glazing points that hold the glass in place. The points are buried in the putty and won't be visible until the putty begins to come out. These points are simply pushed into the wood and can be pried out using a sharp chisel or putty knife to pull them out.

The name of the game here is to get the glass out without breaking it. If you happen to break some glass, don't worry, it's not the end of the world. You can find replacement glass pretty much anywhere.

Action Steps

1. Gently begin working the glazing out with a variety of tools. The paint removal process vibrates the sash enough that any glazing that was loose is now ready to fall out, creating places to exploit with your tools.
2. The joint where the glazing and wood meet has been exposed and it's easy to see where to insert the razor for maximum effectiveness. Work slow and be patient.
3. Once the old glazing putty has been removed, seek out the little metal glazing points that pin the glass in place beneath the putty and remove them. Once ALL of the points are gone, gently pry the glass away from the glazing rabbet.
4. Gently remove the glass, label which opening it belongs in with a marker and set it aside in a safe place.
5. Scrape the glazing rabbets free of any remaining putty so that you have a clean, level surface to reinstall the glass later.

> **PRO TIP**
>
> Part II of this book discusses some options for building your own steam box to make deglazing much easier. Steam also helps avoid glass breakage.

1. Carefully remove old putty

1. Using a chisel to chip out remaining putty

Different types of glazing points you may find

STEP 3
DUTCHMAN REPAIRS

Dutchman repairs may sound complicated, but they are really just shortcuts to avoid replacing an entire element of the window. You cut out the damaged section and glue in a new piece of healthy wood.

Determining whether your window needs a dutchman or epoxy repair is not a science. They can be done interchangeably, and the decision to do one repair over the other depends on personal preference most times. I have included both so that you can make your own decision based on your abilities.

I prefer to use dutchman repairs for larger sections that are fairly straight and simple and I use epoxy for mold-making work to recreate missing profiles and fix rotted joints. Find the way that you are most comfortable with and stick with it. Check out Chapter 17 for more in-depth information about dutchman repairs.

Action Steps

1. Cut the damaged wood section back to sound wood. Make a square cut to make fitting the new piece easier.
2. Cut a piece of wood for the repair that fits into the damaged section, but is slightly larger. Make sure the repair sits proud of the surface to allow for sanding later.
3. Glue in place with Titebond III or similar waterproof exterior grade wood glue and clamp securely for a minimum of 1 hour but a few hours is best. Do not stress glue joints for a minimum of 24 hrs.
4. After 24 hrs. plane or sand down the dutchman until it is level with the surrounding surface.

> **PRO TIP**
>
> Be sure to install a dutchman with the same species of wood if possible and with the wood grain running the same direction as the original.

A proper dutchman after sanding

After painting a dutchman should not be noticeable

Old Windows In-Depth

STEP 4
EPOXY REPAIRS

    This process is just the same as with the window jambs. There is not much that can't be rebuilt with WoodEpox. If you aren't up to milling replacement parts, then large sections can be rebuilt using epoxy and then planed, carved and sanded to match the originals.

    Like I mentioned before, start small with your epoxy repairs while you get used to working with these materials. Once you've gained some confidence working with epoxy, start attacking larger and more complex sections that require attention.

    For wood sash, epoxy is really the only product that is acceptable. Standard wood fillers can be used to fill small holes if needed, but stay away from large repairs using Bondo or other fillers.

    Bondo gets too hard and doesn't move with the wood during seasonal swelling and shrinking, which causes the wood to eventually push the patch out. Strength through flexibility is one of the advantages of a dutchman or epoxy patch.

Action Steps

1. Make sure areas to be repaired with epoxy are dry before proceeding with application.
2. In a disposable container, mix parts A & B in equal amounts of LiquidWood, let sit in the cup for 5-10 mins. before applying to areas requiring repair and portions or wood that need stabilization (ie. slightly soft wood) with a disposable brush.
3. Let LiquidWood setup on the wood for 10-15 mins. Mix parts A & B in equal amounts of WoodEpox until blended well and press into damaged areas while LiquidWood is still slightly tacky. Make sure the repair sits proud of the surface to allow for sanding later.
4. Once the epoxy has cured and has hardened (as little as one hour for large repairs and overnight for small repairs or during cold weather) using a chisel, small block plane or sandpaper level and smooth the surface.

> **PRO TIP**
>
> Wear nitrile gloves, eye protection and drop cloths or plastic around work areas at all times when using epoxies. These are serious fillers, so be cautious of spills.

2. Apply LiquidWood to affected areas

3. Build up missing areas with WoodEpox

4. Shape and sand cured epoxy

STEP 5
SAND & PREP

This is your last chance to take care of any final issues before we start the painting process. Any little divots or rough spots should be smoothed out.

For the flat portions of the sash, I make a quick pass on a random orbit sander with 80-grit paper and then change to 120-grit paper. After that, I prefer to use dowels wrapped in sandpaper or small sanding blocks to carefully sand down the delicate profiles on the interior of the muntins.

Most residential sash are 1 3/8" thick and they need to stay that way. Don't go overboard with the power sander and start taking away wood. If you sand your windows too much, you'll be left with sash that are too thin and rattle in the jambs. A light sanding to smooth things out is all that's needed.

After you're finished sanding, wipe it down with mineral spirits to clear away any remaining dust and prepare the surface for primer.

Action Steps

1. Sand all surfaces with 80-grit sandpaper by hand or gently using a random orbit sander.
2. Repeat process with 120-grit paper.
3. Vacuum off sanding dust and wipe sash down with a rag moistened with mineral spirits.

Carefully sand muntins to protect details

Various size and shape sanding blocks

STEP 6
PRIMING

Priming is the first line of defense for your window, but there are some spots that should be left bare of primer and paint so that they can breathe properly. This technique is a bit controversial, but extensive testing by folks a lot smarter than me have shown that by leaving certain portions of the sash bare, the wood is able to stay dry enough that rot and paint failure can be largely avoided.

It may sound contrary that not painting wood keeps it drier, but the fact is that windows get wet, and if you keep strategic portions bare, you allow the wood to breathe and dry out faster between wettings.

As far as how to properly apply primer, always keep working in one direction. Primers can dry quickly, and if you keep brushing the primer too long, you will be stuck with lots of brush marks to sand down. Put the primer on, smooth it out and leave it alone.

Action Steps

1. Apply oil-based primer with a high quality brush. Brush in thoroughly and lightly "tip off" the surface with your brush to smooth out the finish.
2. Let primer dry for a minimum of 2 hrs. or until it dusts up when sanded.
3. Hand sand sash lightly with fine grit sanding sponge then blow off dust.

Leave these areas free of primer and paint:
- Both sides where the rope mortise is (pictured)
- The very top of the top sash (pictured)
- The very bottom of the bottom sash

> **PRO TIP**
>
> Oil-based primer works best because it seals the wood better and is able to be sanded to a super smooth surface, unlike latex primers.

Old Windows In-Depth

1. Prime with oil-based wood primer

Paint this, NOT that

STEP 7
GLASS PREP

Sparkling clean glass free of all the gunk that has built up over the years is a big part of making your windows really sparkle. Remove any haze or deposits on the glass before reinstalling them in the sash with the steps below.

For stubborn haze and deposits, you can use a rubbing compound designed for glass called CR Laurence Sparkle. This is applied just like waxing a car and does a great job at removing stubborn haze.

Action Steps

1. On a flat surface, lay down a blanket and spray some water on the glass. Wet scrape the glass with a flat razor blade on both sides to remove all residue.
2. Clean glass with glass cleaner and clean rag or paper towel.
3. For hazy glass that doesn't quite come clean, use CR Laurence Sparkle. Buff on with a clean, damp rag, let dry then buff off with a new clean, dry rag.
4. Label individual panes of glass if labels are cleaned off.

Replacement Glass

What do you do if you have broken glass? You can find replacement glass at most hardware stores or any local glass supplier. Use either single strength (3/32") or, better yet, double strength (1/8") glass in your old windows.

You can cut your own glass, but usually it's simplest to measure the opening size and have the store cut it for you if you're not comfortable. Whatever size the opening is, make sure your glass has about 1/16" gap on all sides so it fits without too much pressure, or else you may end up with another broken piece of glass. Check out chapter 14 for more glass options you can use.

Wet scrape glass to prevent dust and protect the glass from scratching

STEP 8
BED GLASS

Bedding the glass refers to installing the glass back into the sash in a bed of putty. This helps air seal the glass and prevents water from getting behind the glass as well.

Any of the glazing points we talked about earlier can be used to set your glass in place. Just make sure they are firmly in place and the glass is where you want it to be before setting your points.

Make sure the glass is evenly set into the puttied glazing rabbet and you only leave a thin film of putty on the interior side of the glass.

Action Steps

1. Dry fit glass into sash to determine the correct orientation. Trim glass if needed.
2. Bed a small amount of Sarco Type-M (or similar) putty in glazing rabbets and gently press glass into bedding.
3. Use a point driver or putty knife to insert at least one glazing point into each side of glass and an additional point every 12". *(Be sure to set point far enough back so that it lays behind the glazing rabbet.)*
4. Remove excess putty from inside of sash and tool interior putty flush and smooth with profile.

> **PRO TIP**
>
> Only press the glass around the edges, especially on large pieces. Pressing on the center of the glass can stress it too much and cause it to break.

2. Bed glass evenly into puttied rabbets

3. Install new glazing points

4. Clean excess putty from the interior

Old Windows In-Depth

STEP 9
FINISH GLAZE

Glazing is the big finish to all of the work you've been doing. Work the putty until you are satisfied with the results. A well glazed window should have clean straight lines of putty and none of it should be visible to occupants from the inside.

Properly installed glazing putty should be installed to a 45° angle to allow it to shed water effectively with mitered corners. I won't lie that this can take some practice to get just right. But, perfectly glazed windows are not necessary for the putty to do its work.

When you first get your putty out, mix it thoroughly to ensure the oils are spread throughout the whole batch of putty. If the putty is cold, you can knead it a bit to help it gain some workability. My preferred putty is Sarco Type-M, but other forms are acceptable, like DAP 33 which is readily available at most hardware stores.

In Step 4 below, I mention using whiting. This is simply ground up chalk and it helps to absorb excess oils from the putty and clean the oil residue that inevitably gets on the glass. You can usually find it at paint stores or online at our store on The Craftsman Blog.

Action Steps

1. Place putty into glazing rabbet.
2. Pack putty firmly in the glazing rabbet and glass junction to get a good seal.
3. Using a putty knife, tool finish glazing at a 45° angle to smooth finish with clean mitered corners. Remove excess putty.
4. Using an old paint brush, apply whiting to inside and outside of glass. Work in thoroughly to remove oil spots from glass being careful not to disturb putty. Blow off remaining whiting.

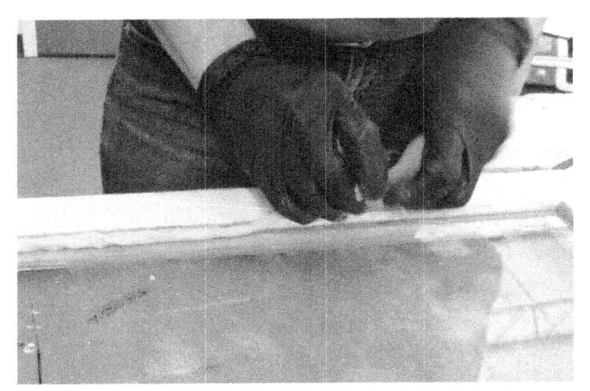

1. Place putty into glazing rabbet

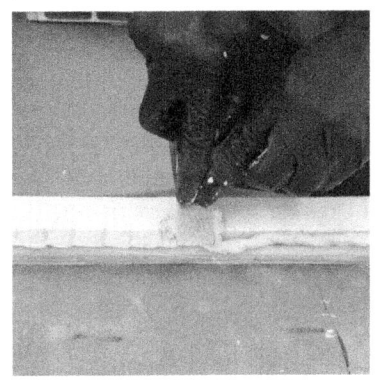

2. Pack putty into rabbet

3. Tool putty to smooth beveled finish

3. Make clean mitered corners

Old Windows In-Depth

STEP 10
FINISH PAINTING

Proper painting is extremely important to making your hard work last. Use the best exterior paint that you can afford. I use exterior grade paint on both sides of the sash since the inside of a sash gets some serious punishment from sun and condensation too.

Use an enamel paint, which has a nice hard finish. Oil-based paints give a great finish, though they can yellow over years and have mildew problems outdoors if you live in a wet climate.

Proper painting of a wood sash will require two full coats on both the inside and outside. The most important part of painting the sash is to lap the paint over the putty and onto the glass just a little bit (about 1/16"). This protects the putty on both the interior and exterior from the elements. Exposed putty will dry out very quickly and fail in a matter of months or at most, a year or two. Properly painted putty will last decades.

The key to making sure that your putty is protected is to paint a straight line by hand without using tape or coming back with a razor blade later. Cutting the paint or tearing off the tape after the paint has dried breaks the paint bond to the glass and the paint will peel back, allowing water and air to get to the putty. This is what you want to avoid at all costs.

Action Steps

1. Once putty has skinned over (3 days to 2 weeks, depending on the type of putty you use) apply two coats of finish paint to both the inside and outside of the sash.
2. The paint must lap past the putty onto the glass approximately 1/16" on both the interior and exterior and must be painted by hand.
3. Allow a minimum of 24 hrs. for paint to dry before reinstallation of sash.

PRO TIP

Don't rush into painting too soon. If your putty hasn't setup long enough to develop a skin, then the paint will not adhere and you'll end up repainting.

Finish paint with your choice of colors

2. Paint MUST lap onto glass at least 1/16"

The results of cutting paint away from the glass

Old Windows In-Depth

STEP 11
RE-INSTALL TOP SASH

The time has come! Your sash are fully restored, your jambs are clean and ready, the hardware is gleaming and you're ready to have a window again instead of plywood. Re-installing the sash is like putting the puzzle back together again. Everything has its place and order.

One thing to be very careful of is the soft putty on the sash exterior. Putty will stay soft for months and is susceptible to gouging during that time. I have seen too many of our windows get glaring fingerprints in the putty when they are being reinstalled. It's easy to forget this portion of the sash that remains fragile. Keep your fingers off of the soft putty or you'll mess up your beautiful work.

Another tip for reinstalling with success is to use a small nail to hold the rope knot in the mortise on the side of the sash. This will give yourself a little insurance that the rope won't slip out inadvertently in the future.

Follow the order of operations below and things should fit back together nicely.

Action Steps

1. Install parting bead for top rail and on the side of the jamb where the stop remains. Parting bead does not need to be nailed in place. It should fit snugly into the channel.
2. Install the upper sash first by pressing the rope knot securely into rope mortise on the side of the sash. Repeat for the other side and swing the sash into place. If knots are loose in mortise, they can be tacked in place with a small nail.
3. Push top sash down onto the sill and install the parting bead on the remaining side by sliding parting bead into place from above meeting rail of the upper sash.
4. Make sure both parting beads are securely set into place using a hammer and a scrap piece of lumber or a rubber mallet.

> **PRO TIP**
>
> Parting bead not fully seated in its channel can make the top sash difficult to move. Make sure the whole length of parting bead is fully installed.

2. Swing sash into place after ropes are attached

3. Install remaining parting bead

STEP 12
RE-INSTALL BOTTOM SASH

Once your top sash is in place, the bottom sash is easily installed. Set the bottom sash on top of the stool and pull the ropes down so that you can insert them in the mortises. Once the ropes are attached, you can swing the sash into place and test the operation of both the top and bottom sash.

If everything is working smoothly, it's time to put the stop on and finish up. Your cleaned up stops should be nailed back into place where they were originally. Unless you have an extremely tall window, each stop shouldn't need anymore than four or five nails to hold it in place.

It's also important to use shorter nails to avoid any long nails protruding into the weight pocket, which can interfere with operation of the weights (a common issue when parting bead is nailed in place).

A good tip to get the right stop placement is to push the bottom sash against the parting bead and insert a putty knife between the bottom sash and stop. Make everything snug and nail the stop in place. Put one nail a couple of inches from the bottom, one at the meeting rail, one a couple of inches from the top and one more in between each of those three nails.

Once the putty knife is removed, it will give you the perfect spacing for your sash. Any looser and you'll have a window that lets in drafts and any tighter will make the window hard to operate.

Action Steps

1. Install lower sash by pressing the rope knot securely into the rope mortise on the side of the sash. Repeat for the other side and swing sash into place. If knots are loose in mortise, they can be tacked in place with a small nail.
2. Reinstall remaining stop using four to five 1 1/4" 18 ga. nails. Stop placement should allow for smooth operation of bottom sash.
3. Ensure smooth operation of both sashes by fully opening and closing both a few times.
4. Wipe down any fingerprints on painted surfaces with a damp rag.

> **PRO TIP**
> If both sash are installed properly, they should move up and down with minimal effort. Two fingers should be enough force to operate the window.

1. Fit knotted end of rope into mortise

2. Insert putty knife between the sash and stop while nailing on stop to properly space window.

Old Windows In-Depth

PART II

WHAT'S NEXT

So, you've walked through the first part of this book, which contains the order of operations for window restoration that I use in my shop every day. Now what? In Part I, I purposely skipped a lot of details that may or may not pertain to your windows and saved them for Part II.

Issues like working with varnish, or deciding between rope or chain, dealing with serious rot or structural damage that require advanced dutchman or epoxy repairs, dealing with alternative balance systems like tapes or spirals, weatherstripping options.

All of those may be scenarios that don't come up every time, but come up often enough that they deserve mentioning are included in this section, along with pictures and tutorials where I felt it would be most helpful.

You may need all of these chapters or none of them, but they are here for you so that when you come up against the unknown, you are ready to take it on. You'll also notice that some of these are more informational like the section different types of glass, and others are strict tutorials with action steps all along the way. I felt that the mixture of information and additional tutorials was the best way to help you accomplish your restoration projects the most successfully.

Also, Chapter 13 is a little different from the rest of the book because it contains the whole process from beginning to end for restoring steel windows should you be the lucky owner of some steel windows. Rather than individual tutorials, this section is very similar to Part I, as it takes you through the whole process from start to finish.

So, dig into these as you see fit to use them as reference or prop the book open on your workbench and follow along the steps as you get those window restored.

CHAPTER 7
WORKING WITH VARNISHED WINDOWS

Often, you'll come across windows whose interior finish is varnish or shellac instead of paint. This poses a couple of challenges, depending on what your future plans are for the sash.

Clear finishes don't provide nearly as much protection from the sun as paints do, and often, the meeting rails and profiles of these sash are weathered considerably, making for longer repair times. A clear finish also makes filling with epoxy or other patching compounds require an artist's touch to help the repair blend in.

Easily repaired sections, when covered with paint, will completely disappear, but not with varnish or shellac. They stick out like a sore thumb and ugly up your work. Here are some tips for working with these kind of sash, whether you plan to paint them or restore them to a natural finish again.

Changing to a Painted Finish

If you're gonna paint it all in the end, then that certainly makes restoration a little simpler. You can do your dutchman and epoxy repairs in a carefree fashion and not worry about anything other than getting a smooth surface.

You'll still need to do a little extra preparation to get the surface ready for priming and painting. Otherwise, your new paint won't look very good or last very long. We'll start with removing as much of the old finish as possible.

Tips for Removing Shellac

I find that most windows with a natural finish inside were originally shellac, which is good news, because shellac is easier to remove than varnish. Shellac can gum up your sandpaper and render it completely useless, though.

To remove it easily without drama, scrub it off with a rag or scratchy pad dipped in denatured alcohol. Denatured alcohol will dissolve hardened shellac with ease. It may take a couple of rounds to get it all, but it is faster than sanding, believe it or not. Once the majority of the finish is off, sand the surface smooth to prep for priming.

Priming Varnished Windows

Priming is an absolute must when changing from a varnished or shellacked interior to a painted interior. Prime with an oil-based primer, which will give you the proper stain blocking and adhesion you need for the finish paint.

Usually, this is sufficient enough to block any old stains from bleeding through, but sometimes you'll be left with dreadful pink streaks!

With tropical woods and old stained surfaces, the old color can bleed right through the primer and turn it pink. Another coat of primer is not the answer. You need to bring out the big guns and use a Shellac-based primer. I know it seems weird to cover old shellac with new shellac, but shellac-based primers are the very best stain blockers out there.

These are not acceptable for exterior use, though. It's a good thing that you'll almost never encounter a window whose outside was varnished, otherwise, blocking the stains would put you in a conundrum.

Apply just one coat where you have the bleed through, or to be safe, cover the whole sash interior if it appearing in multiple locations. These primers are expensive (at over $50 a gallon) so use it sparingly unless you have some money to burn.

Once you've applied the primer, give it a day or two to double check that you have indeed stopped the bleeding. It can take a couple days for the color to make its way through the primer. If it looks good, then you can safely paint like the instructions I laid out in Step 12 of Part I.

Restoring a Natural Finish

One of the most time consuming things to do in window restoration is to remove paint from the inside profiles of the sash. If your sash are not painted, but rather varnished or shellacked, you have just won the lottery in that regard. No scraping paint on the inside, yay!

You will have to smooth out the surface and clean the old finish off before you can apply anything new. Old shellac is especially bad at darkening considerably over decades of use, so removing it will really improve the appearance of the wood underneath.

I recommend starting with the same procedure that I outlined earlier in the "Tips for Removing Shellac" section until you get to nice clean wood. If the finish doesn't respond to the denatured alcohol, then it is likely a varnish of some sort and needs to be sanded down to bare wood. Once you're certain all of the old finish has been removed, you're ready to stain the sash.

Different Order of Operations

I do things in a slightly different order when restoring a stained and varnished sash than a sash that is fully painted. After you have followed the process outlined earlier for removing the old interior finish and the process outlined in Part I for removing the exterior paint, your sash should be repaired and given a final sand as usual.

This is where I change the order of things a bit. On a painted sash, I would normally prime everything at this point, but for a natural interior finish, you want to stain and then apply one coat of varnish on the interior first to protect the finish from any dripping or spilled primer.

The other issue you have when dealing with finishing a natural sash is that we typically prime the glazing rabbets to keep the wood from drawing the oils out of the glazing putty you bed the glass in, but in this case, it's too hard to keep a perfectly clean primer line with absolutely no drips onto the interior. Because of that, I recommend leaving the rabbets bare, priming only the exterior faces of the sash. If a little primer sneaks into a glazing rabbet, it's not a problem unless it runs down onto the interior surface of the sash.

So, how do we handle the issue of the wood drawing the oils out of the putty? There's a simple fix for that. You wipe the rabbets with a rag dipped in boiled linseed oil right before you apply the bedding putty and set your glass. That gives the wood the oil it needs and prevents it from pulling it out of the putty and prematurely drying the putty.

I know that is a lot of changes to my typical process, so below is the order of operations for both natural finish interior and painted sash interior so that you can compare them side by side and see how they differ.

Wipe boiled linseed oil on rabbets

Helmsman Spar Urethane *Epifanes Spar Varnish*

Staining Your Sash

Applying stain is not too complicated, but you have to make sure the wood is completely free of old finish and any sanding dust before applying your stain. If you can safely say the surface is clean and clear, then applying stain is as easy as dipping a rag into the stain of your choice and wiping it onto the interior of the sash.

Let the stain penetrate for just a couple of minutes and then wipe it off with a clean rag. If you want a deeper color, you can apply multiple coats until you reach the color profile that you want. There is a point that the wood won't really accept anymore stain though, so you can only go so far.

Let the stain dry long enough (usually 6-8 hrs) that when you press a rag onto it, you don't get any color transfer.

Choosing the Right Varnish

There are a lot of options for varnish on the market today, and just like any product, some are better and easier to work with than others. At the time of this writing, there are two products that I prefer for windows. Helmsman Spar Urethane and Epifanes Spar Varnish are my two favorites and both will work great. Epifanes is, in my opinion, a superior finish due to its formulation, but it is not as readily available as Helmsman, so the decision is yours. Helmsman seems to be readily available at most hardware store, whereas Epifanes is best found online.

I will also say that there are water-based varnishes and I do not recommend those at this time. The finish is still not up to the same quality as the oil-based products.

Both of the varnishes that I mentioned above are not standard varnish, they are "spar" urethane or varnish, which is a slight tweak to the standard varnish recipe. The long and short of it is that a spar varnish has a couple of characteristics that make it a better choice for windows because it is designed for exterior usage. While your sash interiors are not exposed to the exterior, they are subject to the same heavy UV, weather, and temperature exposure as outdoor wood.

The modified formulation of spar varnishes adds UV blockers to protect the wood and finish. They also have a higher oil content, which creates a softer and more flexible finish that can handle the extreme movement associated with exterior application. Standard varnishes will not last as long and begin to crack and fail in short order compared to a spar varnish, which will provide a longer service life. Whatever brand you pick is up to you and there are plenty of options, I just recommend that you only use a spar varnish on your window sash.

Applying Varnish

Varnish is sometimes a little intimidating for DIYers to apply, though it is much the same as applying any oil-based paint.

Like I mentioned earlier in the order of operations, you'll want to apply your first coat of varnish as soon as your stain is dry. This helps protect the natural finish on the inside from any contamination like primer or glazing putty. Once that first coat of varnish is cured, the wood is sealed and protected so that if you happen to have any primer spills or anything else gets on the surface, they can be wiped off much easier.

The second and third coats should be applied after the glass is bed in place and you can cut in the varnish with your brush right up to the glass to cover the glazing putty.

To apply your finish, make sure you have a good quality brush that is intended for use with oil-based paints or stains. This is usually a natural bristle brush, but there are synthetic options available, it just needs to be acceptable for and oil-based finish, which not all brushes are.

Just like any paint, brush it on smoothly and tip off the surface to make sure your brush marks are minimal. Don't try to work the varnish too much or you will end up with more brush marks than if you had put it on and left it alone. Another helpful tip is to apply your varnish with the sash laid flat since varnish is thinner than paint. This prevents runs and allows the varnish to lay down better and provide a smoother finish.

You may find it beneficial to thin your varnish with mineral spirits to make a thinner finish, which will lay down easier and help you avoid brush marks. If you do thin your finish by more than 10-15% I would recommend adding a fourth coat since the thickness will not be as sufficient as a full strength coat.

Make sure that you give the varnish ample drying time between coats, and unlike paint, you will need to lightly sand between coats with a 220-grit sponge or paper. Dried varnish is a very slick surface and the sanding between coats gives the next coat some tooth to grip onto. Without sanding, it's likely you'll get peeling varnish from a bad bond. After applying the final coat, there is no sanding necessary just let it cure as long as you can afford (at least 36 hrs.) and then you are ready for installation.

> **PRO TIP**
>
> Thin your varnish anywhere from 10% - 25% with mineral spirits for an easier application that will help avoid brush marks and speed drying times.

CHAPTER 8
WEATHERSTRIPPING OPTIONS

There are a TON of options for weatherstripping wood windows. Some of them are are expensive and labor intensive, while others are cheap and easy.

When it comes to choosing the right weatherstripping for your needs, you really do get what you pay for. Metal options like integrated zinc and spring bronze may cost more but they can last for hundreds of years with little or no maintenance.

Less expensive options like peel and stick felt, foam, or vinyl fins often last anywhere from a couple years to a decade max. I'll walk through some of the most popular and readily available options that you have when it comes to weatherstripping old wood windows and how to install them.

Spring Bronze

It's been around for centuries and is one of the most popular and effective weatherstripping options. Spring bronze installed along the sides of the jambs can seal gaps of up to 1/2" reliably and will last almost indefinitely. The bronze ages gracefully to a nice copper patina and is a great options for almost any situation. It does require the sash to be removed in order for installation to be completed, but other than that, installation is fairly straight forward. You can buy it online at our store on The Craftsman Blog.

Spring Bronze

Interlocking Metal

This is proven to be the most effective form of weatherstripping for wood windows. Interlocking metal weatherstripping is ingeniously designed for maximum draft blocking, which is what really counts when it comes to window efficiency. Installation does require removal of the sash and a lot of modification to the sash that may be beyond the abilities of a lot of homeowners. There are pieces interlocking pieces installed along the

Interlocking Metal

perimeter of the jamb and at the meeting rail for maximum efficiency. You'll find options in both bronze and zinc in different locales and both work equally well.

StopGap

This is a simple to install product that we sell at The Craftsman Blog that does wonders at sealing the biggest offender of drafts for double-hung windows- the meeting rail. Even when a wood window is properly installed, there is a certain amount of space that needs to exist in order for the sash to operate smoothly. That extra space is an issue for air leakage at the joint between the meeting rail and parting bead and there is no other form of weatherstripping that can effectively seal this while allowing the sash to still operate except StopGap. The design is also an attractive bronze escutcheon over top a felt gasket so that you can block drafts in style.

StopGap

Vinyl Fins

Some of these fins are as easy and peel and stick and others are inserted into a slot that needs to be cut into the sash. They are available at a lot of hardware stores and also from Conservation Technology in lots of different sizes and designs. Vinyl can last for several years but after many years of exposure, it will eventually become brittle and less effective. This is a good midrange cost option
with a decent lifespan.

Vinyl Fins

Felt

Felt is a great and very affordable option for use in a variety of ways on windows and doors. The wide variety of thicknesses and widths available as well as its ability to be trimmed to any size you need makes it infinitely customizable for any application. Felt weatherstripping can be installed in a couple of different ways. The first is peel and stick, which is as simple as it gets to install. All you need to get this in place is opposable thumbs. The second and more effective and long lasting is nailed in place. Using attractive coppered nails, you can attach felt in a way that it will stay put for a long

Felt

Old Windows In-Depth

time.

Silicone Bulbs

Silicone is a great product for weatherstripping because, unlike rubber or vinyl, it ages very well and maintains its flexibility, despite years of weather and UV exposure. There are some peel and stick silicone bulbs, but the best options are pressure fit into a slot cut into the sash or door. The bulb is a good choice for compression applications but not for sliding scenarios where metal or felt is a better choice since it may tear or cause sticking movement. You can find a wide variety of these at Conservation Technology again.

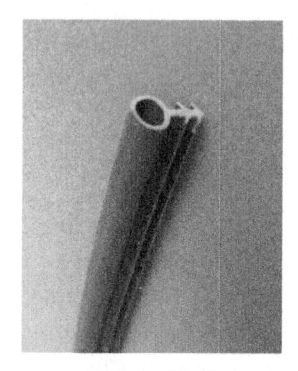

Silicone Bulb

Compression Foam

The compressible foam you can get at most home stores for just a few bucks is as cheap and easy as it gets. It's simple to install and effective for only a short time before it looses its ability to seal an opening, I use it more as a stop gap measure until a more permanent solution can be found. This is almost exclusively found in peel and stick versions. If you're a renter, this is a great option due to its low price and easy reversibility.

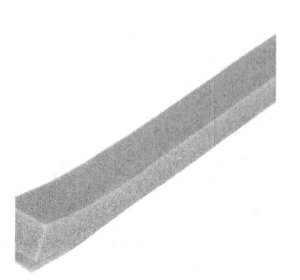

Compression Foam

Rope Caulk

Rope caulk is a little different from the other options we've discussed, because it is designed for seasonal use only, but it is still an important weapon in your weatherstripping arsenal. It comes in an easy to apply roll and feels like firm Play-doh. You just unroll and press it into place around your windows and they are sealed for the winter. While installed, it prevents opening and closing of the window until you peel it off in the spring, but who needs to open a window in January anyway?

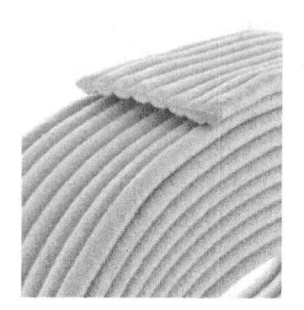

Rope Caulk

CHAPTER 9
INSTALLING & REMOVING WEATHERSTRIPPING

Windows across the country often have some kind of weatherstripping that was previously installed, whether it was original or retrofit at some point in its life. Learning to install your own weatherstripping can make huge energy improvements in your windows.

Likewise, learning how to remove sash on windows that have been previously weatherstripped can require some training to work around the weatherstripping and not damage either the sash or weatherstripping.

In this chapter, we'll look at mainly metal weatherstripping, since that can be the most difficult to work with, especially integrated metal. I have rarely found any problems working around peel and stick or other similar options, so I'll trust that those options are fairly self explanatory.

How to Install Spring Bronze

In my humble opinion, spring bronze weatherstripping is the most effective, and yet still homeowner friendly weatherstripping to install. Sure, it's not as simple as peel and stick foam, but it's a ton more effective.

I'll walk you through the steps to get a successful installation of this lifetime weatherstripping below. Take your time and do it right and you'll never have to mess with it again.

You'll need to have the sash removed from the window jamb in order to install the spring bronze, so follow the instructions outlined in Part I for getting the sash out.

If your windows are painted shut or can barely move due to paint build up, installing spring bronze won't do much good other than to make them even more difficult to operate.

TOOL LIST
- Hammer
- Tape Measure
- Tin Snips
- Drill w/ 5/64" bit
- Nail Set
- 1 1/4" Spring Bronze
- Coppered Nails (coastal regions need solid bronze nails)

If this is the case, prior to installation, scrape the jambs clean of the decades of paint build up so that you have a smooth surface to work with. If you want your jambs primed (which I recommend) or painted, you'll need to do this prior to installation as well. Trying to paint around spring bronze is a pain in the @$#.

If you have restored, easily operable, or even windows that are just loose in their jambs, you are a good candidate for spring bronze weatherstripping. If your windows are caulked shut or impossible to move, you'll have some other restoration work to do before you're ready for spring bronze.

Also, there are multiple widths of spring bronze available from 1 1/8" to 1 3/4". While it is usually standard practice to get the spring bronze that fits the width of your sash (or door) I have found that 1 1/4" spring bronze works just fine for almost all applications, from thick doors to thin sash. It is the most versatile, and the only time I change to something else is for doors or windows that are thinner than 1 1/4" thick.

Step #1 Cut to Length

Measure the height of the bottom sash. Using your tin snips, cut two lengths (one for each side of the jamb). Cut them 1 1/2" longer than the height of the bottom sash with a bevel at the bottom to match the sill angle.

For the top sash, your measurements have to be a little different. Measure the height of the top sash, add 1 1/2" and then measure the distance from the top for the jamb to the bottom of the pulley (in the case of this picture, 9"). Subtract the 9" (or whatever your measurement is from the previous number) and you'll have the length of your bronze for the top sash.

ie. Top sash height = 32" + 1 1/2" − 9" = **24 1/2"**

I promise the math lesson is now over. Phew!

Measure bronze for top sash

Step #2 Pre-drill & Nail

Caution!: Spring bronze is nailed over top of the weight pocket access doors. Once it is installed, it will have to be removed if you ever need to access the weight pockets to change the ropes in the future.

If your jambs are very sturdy and the wood isn't hard as a rock, then you can just nail right through the bronze and into the wood. If you find that the wood is too hard to nail through without bending nails (which is sometimes the case) then you'll need to pre-drill.

- Set your bronze in place on the jamb with the nail side (the flat side) facing inside the house. Make sure it is right in the middle of the jamb. There should be at least 1/16" space between the bronze and the blind stop and parting bead to allow it to flex properly.
- Drill the first hole at the top thru the bronze and into the wood about a 1/2". Tap in a coppered nail so it dimples the surface just a bit.
- Pull the bronze nice and tight and repeat the process about halfway down the length and again at the bottom. The second hole you pre-drill will set the angle of the bronze, so make sure it is lined up straight and doesn't wander into the parting bead or blind stop at one end.
- Go back and repeat the process so that there is a nail every 1 1/2" to 2" along the length of the spring bronze.

Pre-drill and nail up your bronze

Step #3 Spring the Bronze

Once it's all nailed in place, go back and spring the bronze if necessary to increase the amount of gap it will fill. Test fit your window first to see if you have a snug fit or if there are gaps where the bronze isn't running against the side of the sash.

If there are gaps, you need to bend the spring bronze out in those sections so that it puts light consistent pressure on the sides of the sash. To bend the bronze, you can gently use a putty knife to bend it back.

CURVED INSTALLATION OF SPRING BRONZE

If you are one of the select few who have curved windows or doors, don't feel like you're stuck using peel and stick foam or felt weatherstripping if you want the good stuff. Metal weatherstripping, especially spring bronze, is simple to install on curved surfaces with a few tweaks to the installation method.

Jamb or Sash?

The weatherstripping should be installed parallel to the ground and can be nailed onto either the top of the jamb as in the picture (a concave install) or on the top of the sash (a convex install). Convex is always easier, because you're not nailing upside down, but it leaves gaps in the install if the radius of the curve is too tight. Installing on the jamb, while more difficult, almost always yield better results, so that's what we'll talk about here.

How to Install Spring Bronze on Curved Jambs

Kerfed install for arched window

To install spring bronze in an arched top window and door, you start by measuring the length of bronze that you need. Just run a tape measure along the jamb to find your length and add an inch or two to be safe, just like on a regular window. You can always trim the little bit off before nailing in place to make sure it fits exactly how you need it.

Then, before you nail the bronze in place, cut small kerfs half way through the strip every 1 to 2 inches. Just cut through the spring side, not the nailing flange. This will allow the bronze to spring out and overlap a bit, which gives you the best air-sealing you can get. For tighter arches, you may need to cut the kerfs closer together and similarly, for less pronounced arches, you can cut fewer kerfs and space them out further.

Once you are cut and kerfed, then you are ready to to nail in place. Nail off the nailing flange every 1 1/2" and make sure the ends are nailed no further than 1/2" from the edge.

If the wood is too hard and you are having trouble, then pre-drilling is the answer again. Use a 5/64" bit to go through the bronze and jamb and you'll find the install much more satisfying.

For spring bronze and other supplies, see the appendix.

Working with Integrated Metal

Integrated metal weatherstripping is the mac daddy of the weatherstripping world. It is extremely effective, very long lasting, and fairly difficult to work with. Installing new integrated weatherstripping on a window that did not previously have it is beyond the scope of this book, as it requires precise modification of the sash with routers and very careful templating.

However, restoring a window with this type of weatherstripping requires some additional knowledge that I can share with you about how to safely remove and reinstall both the sash and weatherstripping without damaging either. Let's look at what you need to get the job done properly.

TOOL LIST

- Hammer
- Flat Pry Bar
- 5-in-1 Tool
- Needle Nose Pliers
- Nail Set
- Cat's Paw Pry Bar

How to Remove Sash

It would seem that a sash with this type of weatherstripping are permanently stuck in the jamb, but that is not the case. There are just a few more steps before you can remove the sash without damaging it.

The first step to any of this is to have both sash cut free of excess paint or caulk, because the sash need to be able to be moved up and down during this process to access the nails on the metal weatherstrips. So, start with getting the sash at least somewhat moveable again if they are stuck, and then you can proceed with removal.

Step #1 Remove Stops

Just like on any other other sash, remove both interior stops by scoring the paint and prying them off the jamb.

Step #2 Remove Lower Sash & Weatherstrip

Make sure the bottom sash is in the lowest position possible so that you can access the the top portion of the metal weatherstrip on each side of the bottom sash. You should see one small nail at the top of the metal. Slide your flat pry bar or 5-in-1 behind the weatherstrip in this area and gently pry the metal out so that the nail pulls out from the surface a bit. Then, push the metal back, leaving the head of the nail proud of the surface enough that you can pry it off with your cat's paw pry bar or a pair of needle nose pliers.

You have to be gentle with this weatherstripping because it is very thin zinc, which is relatively soft and tear and bend easily.

Once the top nail is removed on both the right and left side of the jamb, raise the lower sash up enough to reveal the lower nails (usually just one or
two toward the bottom) and follow the same procedure above to pull nails out.

If you can't get these nails to pry out, then the fail safe option is to use your nail punch to punch them into the wood through the weatherstrip so that the weatherstrip is now free of the nails. It may have a small nail hole in it, but that won't affect the performance.

Once both weatherstrips are free, you should be able to slide them up over the stool and get the sash out of the jamb along with the weatherstrips. Cut or disconnect the ropes and your bottom sash is free. Label everything so that you know where it goes when you reinstall.

Step #3 Remove Upper Sash & Weatherstrip

Start by removing the parting bead like I outlined in Part I, then make sure the top sash is in the uppermost position and using the same procedure above, remove the two lower nails from the weatherstrip on each jamb. There should be enough space to use a cat's paw to pull the nails out once they are clear enough from the surface.

Lower the upper sash to reveal the two three upper nails, which will be located near the top of the jamb and around the pulley. Pry and remove these nails the same as before from both sides.

Cut or disconnect the ropes and remove upper sash from jamb along with the weatherstrips. Be carful that the weatherstrip does not fall, as it can be harmful to you or to the sill, stool, or hardwood flooring upon impact. Mark the location on the backs of each piece.

Step #4 Restoration of Weatherstripping

Once you have the sash out, you are ready to follow the sash restoration process that I outlined in Part I with a couple of additions. There will likely be an interlocking piece of metal weatherstrip on the meeting rail of both sash that mates when the sash are closed.

I leave these in place because there is no reason to remove them. They can be cleaned up and realigned to make sure that they fit into each other without kinks or other problems. These can be easily bent if you're not careful and before installation, double check to make sure that they are still lined up and free of any paint or other gunk that would impede operation.

I also take this time to clean up the old weatherstripping with 000 steel wool to clean off any paint or dirt and make them more attractive and ease the operation when they are reinstalled. Bend back any kinks and get them ready to go back in.

Step #5 Install Upper Sash & Weatherstrip

Installation is made much easier with a helper to hold things in place. You can do it on your own, but it sometimes feels like you need three hands.

Start by installing both the upper and lower sash weatherstrips on one side of the jamb first (only do one side!) Nail them back where they went using the same or similar sized nails as they were originally attached with and nail in the same locations roughly. Then, install the parting bead on that same side.

Attach the ropes to the upper sash on both sides. Tack the rope in place on the sash with a nail for added security to keep it from pulling out.

While holding the loose piece of weatherstrip in the groove along the edge of the sash, slide the sash into the weatherstrip previously nailed onto jamb and pivot sash into place against the blind stop. The loose weatherstrip should be pushed to the top of the jamb and fit against the weatherstrip on jamb header and nail off the top of the weatherstrip at the top and around the pulley like it previously was attached.

Raise the sash all the way up and nail the bottom portion of the weatherstrip. Insert the remaining parting bead and test the operation of the top sash.

Step #6 Install Lower Sash & Weatherstrip

Following much the same procedure as above, attach both ropes to the lower sash and tack the rope in place with a nail for security.

While holding the loose piece of weatherstrip in the groove along the edge of the sash, slide the sash into the weatherstrip previously nailed onto jamb and pivot sash into place against the parting bead. This time, the loose weatherstrip should be pushed to the bottom of the jamb and fit

> **PRO TIP**
>
> Don't remove the weatherstrip pieces on the top and bottom of the jamb because it is unnecessary. Restore them in place and save the trouble of removal.

against the weatherstrip on sill. Nail off the bottom of the weatherstrip where it was previously attached.

Lower the sash all the way to the sill and put a single nail in the top of the bottom weatherstrip. This one is usually a tight fit, so a nail set is best for getting this nail fully set.

Check that all nails are fully set but not punching through any of the weatherstripping.

Install the two interior stops and then test the operation of both sash to ensure that you've got a smooth up and down. If you need to tweak the fit of the interlocking pieces on the meeting rail so the sash close fully, this is a good time. Also, it's possible that the alignment is not perfect for the sill and header piece of weatherstripping that you left in place. They may also need to be tweaked a bit as well.

Check out the pictures on the following page to see photos of the important parts of the work.

2. Punch nail to remove lower sash

3. Pry nails below top sash

4. Restore bottom & top in place

5. Install upper sash

Detail of nailed strip for top sash

Old Windows In-Depth

103

Chapter 10
Repairing & Replacing SubSills

There are many slight variations of window sill designs over the last couple hundred years, but essentially, most windows either have an integrated sill (which contains the sill and subsill in one thick piece of wood) or a separate sub-sill beneath the window sill proper. Either way, these horizontal exterior portions of the window are subject to severe weathering and rot due their increased exposure.

In Part I, I talked through repairing jambs and sills with epoxy, but sometimes the sill is beyond repair and needs replacement. If this is the case, these tutorials will guide you through the process. Time to channel your inner carpenter.

TOOL LIST
- Safety Glasses
- Multi-Tool
- Reciprocating Saw
- Pencil
- Tape Measure
- Wood & Bi-Metal Blades
- Rot-resistant Wood

Integrated SubSills

To replace an integrated sill, you'll first need to raise the bottom sash so that it is out of the way of your work. It may take some cutting free of paint and caulk, but once you have it safely out of the way, you're ready to begin the removal process.

Start by cutting the nails between the sill and stool. There should be 3 or 4 finish nails here, but there could be any number if the carpenter was mean or bitter. Using a small pry bar, pry the stool up just a bit to gain access to the nails. Then slide your hacksaw in and cut through each of the nails. You may also have some nails running from the side trim down into the sill that need to be cut but this is rare.

Next, using the tool of your choice, either a reciprocating saw, hand saw, or multi-tool, you need to cut a 3-4" chunk out of the center of the sill. I prefer the reciprocating saw for the bulk of the cut and then the multi-tool to finish cleanly. You are making to cuts here so that you can pull the middle 3-4" chunk out of the opening.

The underside of the sill may be notched to accept the siding, so you'll have to cut that free as well if it doesn't seem to move.

Once you have the center notch out, it's usually just a matter of wiggling and pulling and prying to get each of the two remaining sides out. These sides will typically be rabbeted into the jamb and nailed in place. So, it will take some muscle, but with a little patience, it will come out.

Integrated Sill Replacement

Then for replacement. I'd love to give you the specifics for how to make a replacement sill, but with the countless varieties, it wouldn't be much good except for the few of you who have the exact design that I make. Because of that, I feel like a general guide to how to make and install will be most helpful.

The big items you need to be sure to duplicate are the angle of the sill, thickness of the sill, and the proper width.

Too wide and it won't fit in the opening, too narrow and you leave gaps for water to get in. If the angle isn't right, then you won't have a good seal between the bottom sash and sill. And lastly, if the thickness, especially at the inside, is off, then it won't fit beneath the stool properly.

All those items may sound imposing, but the easy part is that you don't have much math to do. You have the old sill you just pulled out to use a template, so use that to your advantage.

There are no complex tools that you need. I can make a replacement sill on just a table saw by using the old sill to set the blade height and angle fairly easily. Use a good rot resistant wood like Western Red Cedar, Cypress, Heart Pine or other regional choices to make sure that your repair lasts.

To install your replacement sill, it's a matter of slowly sliding it back into place. You may have to cut a bevel on the back side of the bottom to allow it to fit into its new home. Make sure that you have a

Deteriorated sub sill needing replacement

> **PRO TIP**
>
> Save your old subsill and use it as a template for making your replacement subsill to make replication much easier.

nice snug fit with overlaps where they used to be and everything looks like it should before nailing it back in place.

You should nail through the stool into the sill as it was before, and then I prefer to screw in through the face of the sill on either side into the framing if you have access. This will usually take a 3-4" exterior screw to penetrate deep enough.

If you don't have access on the sides, you can screw down the the horizontal potion into the rough sill 2x4. If you do this, make sure to countersink the screws and epoxy the holes so that no water will penetrate here. Then, like all repairs, prime, caulk, and paint and you have a new lasting sill.

Separate SubSills

This design is easier to remove and replace than the integrated sill. First, you don't need to get the bottom sash open to complete this replacement. If it's painted shut, it's a problem for a different day. To remove an independent sub-sill, you'll need to cut any nails between the sub-sill and sill, and then cut the nails between the sub-sill and side trim. Nails are more common here for this design.

Once these nails are cut, you can usually slide the sub-sill out with a little oomph and encouragement.

Removal

Separate sub-sills look like a big fat "T" usually. You'll have to measure the proper width, thickness, and angle like in an integrated sill, but this time you have to cut dog ears. The width of the sub-sill has two measurements:

1. The inside of the jamb from left to right
2. The width from the outside of the left casing to the outside of the right casing + 1" (the +1" assumes the sub-sill extends past the exterior casing about 1/2" on either side. If your situation has a large or small reveal than 1/2" then adjust the measurement accordingly)

The difference between these two measurements will determine how wide your dog ears will be. For example, if #1 is 28" and #2 is 39" then that leaves me with 11" remaining. So, each dog ear will be 5 1/2" wide. Make sense?

Installation

This time, you only have to screw through the sub-sill face into the side framing with 3" or 4" screws. Countersink and fill the holes, then prime, caulk, and paint and you are good to go. You don't want to screw down through the sill into the new sub-sill because that creates a super highway for water to penetrate and rot your work.

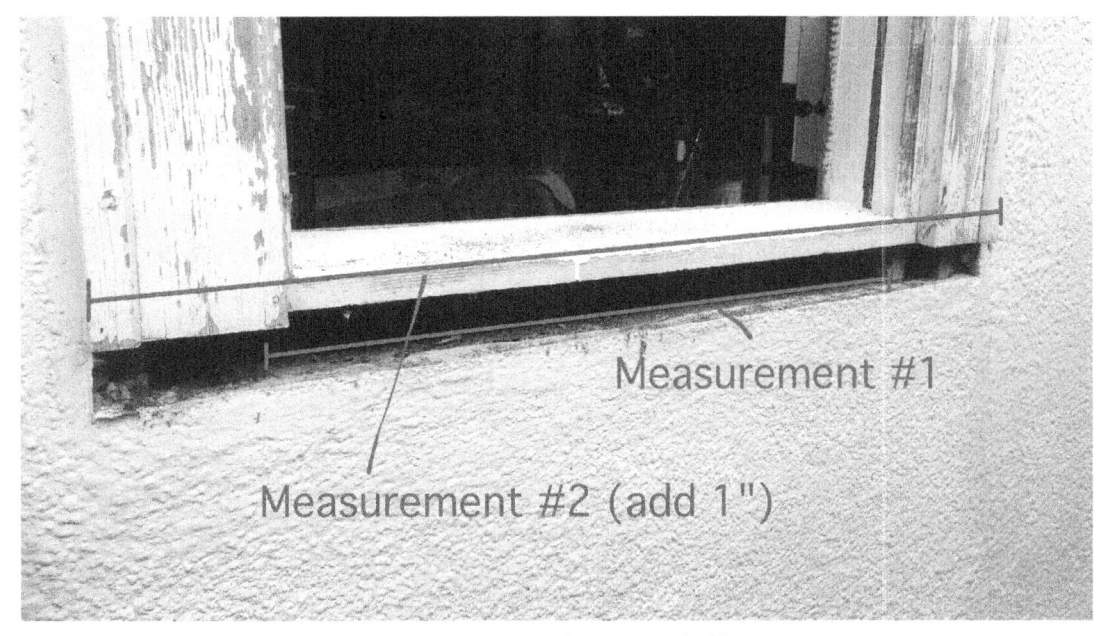

How to measure for a new sub sill

The "fat T" shape of a sub-sill

Cut any remaining nails

Cross section of separate sub-sill

Old Windows In-Depth

CHAPTER 11
CASEMENTS, AWNINGS & HOPPERS, OH MY!

While double hung windows may be the most common type of historic window, there are a lot of other types that fit the historic landscape. Knowing a little about each of these types can help you navigate some of their problem spots and differences.

The process to restore the sash on almost any window is very much the same, but the mechanicals and type of function they offer are what usually define each of these different types.

I'll go into a little detail about each a few of the most common types of windows, but this is by no means comprehensive. There have been windows for millennia and including every type under the sun wouldn't be useful. If you happen to have a type of window not included in this list, I apologize and can only hope that from these discussions, you can figure out the details. As my father says, "I'm not going to let something without arms beat me." I know you can do it!

CASEMENT WINDOWS

Of all of these alternates of windows, casements are probably the most common. Casement windows are a unique animal that seem simple, but can turn into a real pain at times. They are part window and part door and anyone who has ever installed a door will tell you that hanging a door properly is no easy task.

While the restoration process for a casement sash is almost exactly the same as the process I outlined for double hung windows in Part I, casement windows suffer from the same issues that doors do. They sag, bind, twist, and warp in ways that make them particularly drafty at times.

Below are a few things that you should know if you plan to restore casement windows in your house about how to make the hardware work for you instead of against you.

Hinges

The hinges are the most important part of a smooth operation. Casement hinges are exposed to the elements and often caked with paint and rust that needs to be removed.

The first thing to do is to get them cleaned up using the process I outline in chapter 3 of Part I. Once they are cleaned and restored, any ferrous metal should be coated with a rust insisting treatment like Penetrol, boiled linseed oil, or other rust inhibiting clear sealers. I have even brought some hardware to a local powder coating company for ultimate protection, which I highly recommend.

The next issue that you'll run into is stripped screws and loose hinges. From years of abuse, a lot of the screw holes have been stripped out and need to be filled in order to give the screws the holding power that they need to hold the sash in place.

You can fill these old screw holes with wood scraps or epoxies like Kwikwood to help the screws grab hold. Installing new screws that are a little longer (1/4" to 3/4") than the originals is a good idea too since they will grab into fresh wood.

Latches & Operators

There are a thousand different types of latches and operators available for casement windows, so trying to go through them all isn't really feasible, but there are some items that need to be addressed.

First, most operators, whether they be cranks or slides, usually reside on the bottom of the sash, resulting in a tight seal at the bottom and big gap at the top. This issue can be resolved by adding an additional surface bolt or latch at the top of the sash. I find that most leaky casements (air and water) can be resolved with this simple addition.

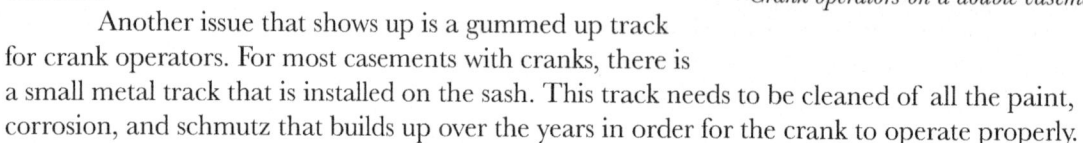

Crank operators on a double casement

Another issue that shows up is a gummed up track for crank operators. For most casements with cranks, there is a small metal track that is installed on the sash. This track needs to be cleaned of all the paint, corrosion, and schmutz that builds up over the years in order for the crank to operate properly.

Sometimes if the sash has sagged or the house has settled, this track may also have to be adjusted to accommodate the sash properly and avoid binding. It's not complicated work, but it can be tedious getting these cranks working smoothly.

If your casement hardware is driving you absolutely batty, then it may be time to simplify. Complicated mechanical cranks can be removed and replaced with just a simple latch at the meeting rail and surface bolt to secure things. Don't be ashamed if you can't get a smooth operation, because even the pros are frustrated enough with casements that we will go back to this simpler system.

AWNING WINDOWS

Wood awning windows are pretty rare, but they can come up from time to time. An awning window is one where the bottom of the sash swings outward and the top stays in place. Awning windows always open outward, unlike casement and hopper windows which can swing either way.

This allows the window to be opened even during rainy weather without allowing water into the house, which was important before the days of air conditioning.

In my experience with them, I usually find them to be one sash per opening, but occasionally, I have come across a double sash awning window.

The hardware for an awning windows can be much the same as a casement since it is basically just a casement turned on its side but with the double sash awning the hardware can be much more complex than just hinges and a crank or stay. I'll discuss the mechanics of one of these more complex double awning windows below.

Double Awning Windows

These double awning windows are unique, but they do show up from time to time, so I felt it worth showing some pictures of the hardware and outlining a little bit about how they work and how you can go about removing the sash for restoration should you need.

I'm sure there are variations on this hardware out there, but other than the simple awning window with a hinges and a stay, this is the only other set of mechanicals I have come across. Let's take a look.

Operation

This type of double awning windows is extremely stable, in my experience. The hinges are placed on the top corners of each sash and are both mortised into the sash and wrap from the inside of the sash all the way around to the front of the sash.

Double awning windows

Both sash are then connected to a crank running across the whole sill, which opens both sash simultaneously with a thin metal tube running vertically on each side to connect the cranking mechanism to the hinges.

Removal of Sash

While you can remove the entire mechanical assembly by simply unscrewing every screw you come across, I have found that unless absolutely necessary, removing the crank and tubes is unnecessary. Removing the crank, tubes, and hinges creates a lot of work on the installation to make sure everything lines up properly and the sash close tight.

That being said, I prefer to simply unscrew the hinges from the sash in order to remove the sash. This results in the mechanicals staying exactly as they are so that you can be guaranteed that reassembly of everything will result in a smooth operation. There are still quite a few flat head screws that strip easily, so clear the paint off of them and use a little WD-40 or other lubricant to get them spinning again.

If your mechanicals are gummed up with decades of paint, then full removal may be necessary in order to get them working again.

Interior crank, tubes and hinges

Remove hinge screws

Mechanical Restoration

The mechanics are usually galvanized steel on these windows, so after 70-100 years of exposure, they usually have accumulated some rust, if not a couple dozen coats of paint. If you are dealing mainly with rust, then cleaning with Ospho rust treatment and some 0000 steel wool should get you a nice clean finish while leaving the mechanicals in place. Then, be sure to coat with a clear finish, like spray lacquer or BoeGuard to protect them from rust going forward.

If they are covered with paint, then after removal, the crock pot method of boiling the paint off is a better option to begin with before treating the rust as above.

Installation of Sash

No surprise here, but putting the sash back is just a matter of screwing them back onto the hinges. A few tips apply, though. First, the purist in me says to use the same flat head screws, but the realist recommends using an impact driver and new Phillips screws because you don't have three hands. Without an impact driver or helper, you will need to hold the sash in place (perfectly lined up with the screw holes) with one hand, hold the screw with the other and then somehow find a third hand to operate your screw driver. Trust me, it's easier with a driver and a magnetic bit.

Stand on the exterior of the window and crank the mechanicals open as far as they go to start with the top sash. Slide the sash up and into the hinge mortises and attach the single screw on the exterior of the sash to line it up before installing the remaining screws on the inside of the sash.

Repeat the same process for the bottom sash once the top is completely screwed off, working from underneath the window. Test the mechanicals and make sure both sash line up and close properly.

HOPPER WINDOWS

Hopper windows are basically the opposite of an awning window with the ability for the top of the sash to to move outward or inward, depending on the design.

The hinges are placed on the bottom and the operator on the top. A lot of operable transoms above

Hopper Window

doors are essentially hopper windows. Their main function is to allow warm air to escape a room and maintain airflow between rooms or the outside.

Often, you will find these small pulls at the top of hopper windows to secure them when closed. The biggest challenge with hopper windows is that if the latch is not in good shape or lined up properly, they can have a tendency to fall open a little or a lot. This obviously isn't good for your energy efficiency, so, getting that top latch lined up so that it closes securely is key with this type of window.

If needed, you can add additional hardware like a surface bolt to keep the window securely closed.

Single Hung Windows

Down here in Florida, I don't get a lot of experience with single hung windows. They are an older form of window that is much more common in the older parts of the country like New England.

So, I invited my friend Alison Hardy of Window Woman of New England and President of the Window Preservation Alliance (WPA) to help me put together this section to make sure I didn't miss any of the nuances of single hung windows that she knows so well from working on some of the oldest windows in America.

Her company is located in Amesbury, MA and does hundreds of single hung windows every year, dating back to before our country's founding.

A single hung window looks just like a double hung window – there is an upper sash and a lower sash. The lower sash is moveable, but the upper sash was not built to move. Single hung windows were made before the advent of weights and pulleys, so, it usually does not have any counter balance system.

There are some instances where single hung windows were modified to have weights and pulleys, but usually it is only to operate the lower sash. More typically,

Single hung window

you will find some sort of catch mechanism to hold the lower sash open.

Single Hung Mechanicals

Removing the sash from a single hung window is a little different from a double hung window, but there are still a lot of similarities.

The first 3 steps of Prep, Stop Removal, and Bottom Sash Removal are all the same, except that you probably don't have ropes to disconnect from the sash. If you have a button catch on the side, you may have to push it in to get the lower sash to raise up.

Step 4 Remove Back Stop

In Part I, Step #4 is parting bead removal, but on single hung windows, there is usually no parting bead. So, this is where things get a little different. What you will find instead is a piece of wood, usually ½" thick that runs from the sill to the bottom of the upper sash that is the same width as the sash. This is called the back stop. You may or may not have to remove these to get the upper sash out. Try without removing the back stop first, but if it feels too stubborn or like you are really having to force things, then it's best to remove the back stop.

To remove the back stop, insert a pry bar under the middle of the back stop and aim to get the wood to lift. You should be able to see how wide it is and you may need to score the paint to the outside window trim, the window casing. If you start from the middle, you can bow it out and then pry forward the bottom and remove it. You may need to score the paint where the back stop hits the bottom of the window. The back stop is usually held in with one or two nails, so it should come out fairly easily.

Removed and cleaned backstop

Step 5 Remove Top Sash

The top sash is most likely heavily painted, caulked around the edges, etc. And imagine the heavy buildup of paint on the outside of the upper sash. Start by cutting around all the edges as described in Part I, then grab the bottom corners of the upper sash and pull them towards you. Rock it in and out if it starts to budge. Gently! You run the risk of having the sash bend in the middle and break lots of glass and sometimes the wood.

If you are having a good day and working gently but firmly, you can rock the upper sash until the back edge of the meeting rail is in front of the back stop. It does not have to be very far, just a tiny bit in front. Then, you can pull in a downward motion. You will probably have to re-score the top edge paint again to free the top edge.

While stopping to do this, if you don't have any safety glasses on, you will want to put them on now. When you release the upper sash, you will probably find a whole lot of dirt. The dirt of ages, the dirt that has accumulated since the sash went in over a century ago. This dirt will aim directly at your eyes, so PROTECT THEM NOW.

If you have not been successful at getting any motion from your upper sash (and really, I was giving you the gold star day scenario, not the typical one) it is time to go back to Step 4 and remove the back stops.

> **PRO TIP**
> Remove the back stop only if necessary to save yourself the additional work and possibility of breaking this thin piece of wood.

Once you have removed both back stops, grab the lower corners of the upper sash and GENTLY but firmly pull the sash towards you. Usually a 5-in-1 tool or a small prybar can get the sash separated from the gobs of paint on the outside. Once you can rock the sash towards you, it's time to pull downwards. Again, lots and lots of dirt will be on the top of the sash, so wear eye protection.

Sometimes the upper sash fits into a slot at the top of the window and getting the outside paint to break free can be a challenge. It's best to work slowly but persistently to rock the sash backwards and forwards and keep pulling down. You might need a prybar at the top to get it to move downward. It will come out. We always win.

Step 6 Installation of Top Sash

Reinstallation is where single hung windows are so wonderful! The upper sash goes in just by sliding it into the opening and pushing it all the way back and all the way up. No ropes other balances to mess with.

While holding the top sash in place, reinstall the back stops (hopefully those have been stripped of all paint or made new) by wedging it under the upper sash and then pressing the bottom into place. It should snap right back into place. You only need 2 or 3 nails to hold it in place once set.

Step 7 Installation of Bottom Sash

The lower sash just drops into place. If you have a side catch, slide the side of the sash with the catch on it in first and then push the other side into place. You can also place the lower sash up high and slide it down into place, pushing the catch in as you go. Put the interior stops on again and you are done!

CHAPTER 12
CHAINS, ROPES, & WEIGHTS

The traditional mechanical balances of historic windows are an example of simple elegance. A rope or chain attached to a hidden weight that perfectly balances the sash allowing it to remain open in any position. It's simple and effective and leaves little room for complications that can foul things up.

I wrote about how to change ropes out in Part I, but here are still some nuanced questions and hacks I can give you here to help you pick the right rope or chain and also smooth out the operation of problematic windows.

CHAIN OR ROPE?

Should I use rope or chain for my windows? This is a big question for a lot of homeowners and the answer is usually very simple. If your windows originally had rope, then stay with rope and if they originally had chain, stay with the chain. The reason is not because I'm a purist, but rather a few reasons that may make more sense once I explain it a bit more.

Window pulleys are designed specifically for either chain or rope, and while they can function with either, they work best with their intended material. Pulleys designed for chain have a flat wheel, whereas pulleys designed for rope have a curved wheel.

The curved wheel cradles the rope better, causing smoother operation and less stress and wear on the rope. The flat wheeled pulleys for chain give the chain nice flat surface to ride on. When you put chain on a curved pulley, it rides mostly on the edges, causing uneven wear and rougher operation.

In many ways, chain is an upgrade. It's more attractive, longer lasting, and can hold more weight than average rope, but these aren't always a major concern and the higher cost of chain is also a factor.

Sure, chain lasts longer but good quality sash rope can last more than 60 years. That's plenty long enough for me to not worry about replacing ropes but once in my life. Don't get me wrong, I love the appearance of sash chain, but rarely is it necessary.

Choosing the Right Rope or Chain

The first thing you need to determine is if you will be going with chain or rope and then we can get into which size and style to choose. Like I mentioned earlier, there are pulleys that are designed to work better with chain and pulleys that are best used with rope. You can interchange them, but I would allow the type of pulley to dictate whether you should use rope or chain.

Which Rope is Right?

A lot of people worry that rope won't be strong enough to support their heavy sash and sometimes this is a problem. How much weight can sash rope hold? The working strength of #8 Samson Spot Cord (which is what I mostly use and recommend) is 150 lbs. that means that anything less than a 300 lbs. sash (remember there are 2 ropes supporting the sash) should be just fine with this rope. Other ropes don't have nearly the strength of Spot Cord.

Samson also makes larger sash cord in sizes #10 through #16 which can hold 480 lbs. to 1080 lbs. respectively. So, really no matter how big the sash is, you can use rope. The larger sash ropes may have trouble fitting in smaller pulleys, so it's best to check sizes and clearances first.

If you don't like the trademark red spot that comes on Samson Spot Cord, there are a lot of other options on the market that can work instead. The main thing in selecting sash rope is to choose a cotton rope with the proper weight rating for your sash. Synthetic ropes are not a good choice because they can stretch, causing the weights to bottom out and the sash to not stay put. Synthetic rope also does not hold up to the intense UV exposure windows are exposed to and will deteriorate faster than cotton.

> **PRO TIP**
> Avoid synthetic ropes like nylon or polyester. They tend to stretch, causing sagging sashes. Sash rope should be high quality cotton rope, which fairs better.

Which Chain is Right?

Sizing chain for residential windows is typically #25, #8, or #829 which have a weight load of between 70 lbs. and 80 lbs. If you're wondering what the numbers mean, I honestly don't know, as it has never been necessary for me to find out, other than to know which number is the right size chain for my windows.

Rarely is there a need for a heavier duty chain, unless you are dealing with very large commercial windows, which can use #3, #35, #45. These chains have a higher weight limit (between

100 lbs. and 175 lbs.) and a larger diameter, so they often do not fit in standard residential pulleys, as they were intended for larger commercial applications.

The material, whether it be bronze, copper plated, stainless steel, or any other option, is less an issue of strength and more of cosmetic preference. I prefer either stainless steel or solid bronze because plated chains can wear and rust with age. There are companies selling a myriad of different chain options to help you find something that suites your needs. Here are a couple of places you can find quality sash chain:

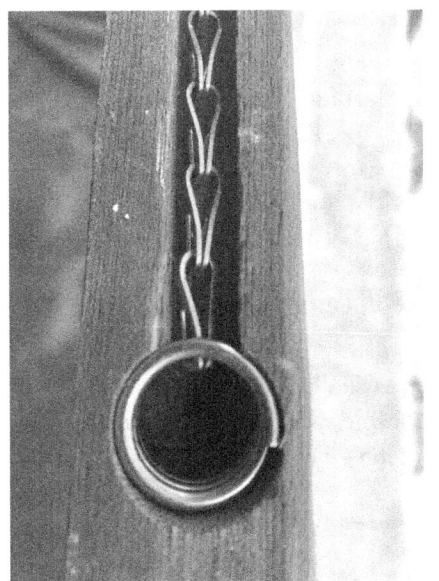

- Kilian's Hardware
- SRS Hardware
- House of Antique Hardware
- Architecture Resource Center

Chain spiral

Chain can be attached either simply or elegantly to sash. It can be as simple as running the chain into the rope mortise on the side of the sash and nailing it in place. A more attractive method for attaching chain to the sash is to use chain spirals, which slot into the rope hole mortise and the chain is then thread onto the ring just like putting keys on a key chain.

The same applies to attaching chain to the weights. You can tie a knot, just like with rope, or use a more attractive method of a chain hook which attaches one side of the chain into another. You loop the chain through the eyelet on the weight and crimp it back onto itself.

WORKING WITH SASH WEIGHTS

Sash weights are not complex. They were usually made of either iron or lead and are hidden so their appearance isn't of much concern, only their function. When you have missing weights, there are lots of options for finding replacements. Some of them are sexy and painted beautiful colors like Tiffany Blue (my wife's favorite color) while others are utilitarian and ugly.

It really doesn't matter which you choose, as long as the replacement is the right weight for the sash. To find the right weight for your sash, each weight should be approximately half the weight of the sash. Say your sash weighs 10 lbs. that would mean a 5 lbs. weight on each side will give it perfect balance.

There is some tolerance to this rule in that you can usually get away with being off by about 10%. So, a 14 lbs sash might be perfectly balanced with two 7 lbs. weights but it will also work satisfactorily with a 7 lbs. and 6 lbs weight or a 7 lbs. and 8 lbs. weight most times. If you can't find the right size weight laying around, you may be able to get away with something close.

Replacement Weights

The first place I'll check for replacement weights is the local architectural salvage yard. They are usually laying in a field and cheap at about $.25 to $.50 per pound. If you don't have access to a salvage yard locally and you can't find any curbside from people replacing their old windows (Grrrr!) then you can buy some from online suppliers like below.

- Kilian's Hardware
- SRS Hardware
- Architecture Resource Center
- Mars Metal
- Architectural Iron Company

There are a lot of options out there, but ordering online can be expensive because of shipping costs on such a heavy product. Some good DIY options are also available.

- Bar Stock - You can contact a local welder or machinist and buy bar stock (preferably round) cut to whatever size/weight you need and have them weld an eyelet on the top of each piece so that you can attach your rope or chain.
- PVC - I have seen a replacement weight made by cutting a length of capped PVC filled with sand, shotgun pellets, or anything else heavy enough to get the desired weight.

These last couple of options may sound pretty ghetto, but it really doesn't matter what you use as long as it fits into the weight pocket and is the right weight. It's just a hidden ballast and anything can function well, as long as it weighs the right amount and won't get hung up in the weight pocket.

Old Windows In-Depth

One last tip about weights- weights usually come in either a square or tubular configurations and I have found that square weights have a greater tendency to get hung up or clank in the pockets. If at all possible, I recommend choosing a tubular shape for smoother operation.

CUTTING WEIGHT POCKETS

Sometimes builders installed their old wood windows without weight pocket access doors to save a couple bucks. While it didn't seem like a big deal at the time, it creates a whole lot of work for us today when you need to change a rope or chain.

Rather than being stuck with the typical alternative of removing the window trim and leaving yourself with a lot of plaster repair, here is an easier way to fix the problem for good.

In this tutorial, you'll learn how to cut weight pocket access doors yourself so that whenever you need access to the hidden weight pocket in the future, you can easily get in there.

It only takes a few minutes per window and you need a couple of tools.

In order to cut the access doors, you'll have to have the sash out of the opening first, but you've already learned how to do that from Part I, right?

Step 1 Measure

Run your tape from the window sill up the side of the jamb. You'll need to make two marks, one at about 9" above the sill and the other about 24" to 28" above the sill. I try to keep the top of my access doors below the top of the bottom sash for reference.

Step 2 Mark Your Cuts

Using a speed square, draw a straight line across the inside portion of the jamb at each of the marks that you made in Step #1 using the blind stop as a straight edge. You'll need to mark the half of the jamb from the parting bead channel to just under where the interior stop goes.

TOOL LIST
- Safety Glasses
- Circular Saw
- Multi-Tool
- Pencil
- Tape Measure
- Speed Square
- 3/4" #8 screws

Old Windows In-Depth

Step 3 Cut Tops and Bottoms

Using the multi-tool, make a plunge cut into the top and bottom marks on the jamb as shown in the picture below. It is imperative that you cut at a different 45° angle for the top and bottom. Attaining a perfect 45° is not crucial, but the direction that the angle goes is. Here is the breakdown:

- The top cut should be at a DOWNWARD angle.
- The bottom cut should be at an UPWARD angle.

Cutting at these two angle creates a trapezoid, which cannot fall back into the hole that you will create. This is the most important part, so pay careful attention.

Step 4 Cut the Sides

Time to break out your circular saw. I used a corded model in this tutorial, but the little battery powered ones are much easier for this. Why didn't I use one? Because someone (me) forgot to load it in the truck the morning we were taking pictures!

Anyway, set the depth on your circular saw to just over 3/4" since most jambs are made of wood this thick. If your house is older than the 1890s, then you may have 7/8" or even 1" thick jambs. If that's the case, you'll need to change the depth.

You may ask why I don't just set the depth to 1" or 1 1/2" to cover all my bases? Because there are lead or iron weights sitting right behind the jamb and I don't want my saw blade to be hitting those big metal weights and create damage and sparks. Start at the shallowest cut and if it doesn't work, keep creeping up on the thickness until you find the right depth.

You'll need to make 2 vertical plunge cuts. *If you've never made a plunge cut using a circular saw before, do a little research to make sure you are doing it safely.* The first should be inside the parting bead channel or rabbet. This cut needs to connect the bottom and top lines you just cut with the multi-tool.

The second vertical line should be located underneath the interior stop so that it is hidden when the window is reinstalled. On this cut it's important to leave at least 1/2" to 3/4" of space between the inside edge of the jamb and the cut. This way you don't compromise the strength of the jamb.

Step 5 Remove & Add Screws

After these two cuts are finished, your new access door should fall right out. If it is still resisting removal, then check that there are a few places you may not have cut all the way through yet.

Once it is free, you can change out the ropes freely. When you're ready to close things up, you'll need to add two 3/4" screws (one at the top and one at the bottom) to secure the door in place until the next time that you need to open it.

I always pre-drill the holes because the screws are so close to the ends of the access door, which greatly increases the chance the wood will split if you don't. Trust me, it's worth the extra 20 seconds.

Step #1 Measure

Step #2 Mark your cuts

Step #3 Cut bottom

Step #3 Cut top

Step #4 Cut sides

Step #5 Remove & add screws

Old Windows In-Depth

4 Hacks for Roping Windows

Re-roping your windows is discussed in Part I, but people are always looking for more ideas on how to make roping easier. So, in this book, I thought I'd share some hacks I've developed to make the process easier.

Hack #1 The Piggyback

If you've still got a rope poking through the pulley, then you can cut the knot off and tape the new rope to the end of the old rope. That way, when you pull the weight out of the pocket, it will easily draw the new rope down the pulley and out of the pocket door. Then you just cut the old rope off the weight, tie the new rope on, and cut it to length. Voila!

Hack #2 The Quick Draw

Don't break out your tape measure, just run a length of rope from the top of the jamb to the sill and cut. That length should be more than enough to tie your weight off and leave some excess for the sash knot.

This trick only works on normal height windows. Any window shorter than about 40 inches may need 2-4 additional inches added to the length of the rope.

Hack #3 The Sinker

When the rope just won't go down the pocket and keeps getting hung up on something, tape a screw to the end before threading it down the pulley. The extra weight encourages it to fall down where it belongs. A little shaking and dancing (of the rope, not your booty) helps the job go easier too.

Hack #4 The Nuclear Option

If you just cannot get the rope to go where it needs and you've tried everything, it may be time for the nuclear option. Cut the paint line at the interior casing and gently pry it off, being careful not the damage the plaster. Once it's off, you'll have full access to the whole weight pocket and you can fix whatever is causing the rope to get stuck. Sometimes it's trim nails in the wrong place that can be cut off, other times it's poorly placed framing. Whatever it is, fix it now and test before putting the casing back on.

CHAPTER 13
PAINTING OPTIONS

There are a ton of products available for painting windows today. Just like there are plenty of good options for painting and finishing windows, there are a lot of bad options too. In this section, I'll walk you through the basics of picking the right paint and help you understand why.

Windows and doors are the only items in a house that are operable, and because of that, they require a special type of paint. A standard latex house paint can cause your windows to gum up and get stuck permanently. So, what kind of paints work best for windows? There are a few different types.

TYPES OF PAINTS

Oil-based Enamels

These have been the standard for decades because traditional oil-based enamels cure to a very hard and resilient finish.

These paints give the finest finishes, in my opinion. They level perfectly due to their slower drying time and can result in a near flawless surface if applied, even with minimal experience.

Once cured, the paint is extremely resistant to blocking, which is a situation where two painted surfaces stick to each other and cause damage to the surface. Blocking causes more windows to get stuck together and painted shut than anything else, so it is to be avoided at all costs, and that is one of the reasons that they have retained their popularity.

Oil-based enamels have some down sides though. They are very slow to dry, 8 hrs to touch and 24 hrs to re-coat typically, with about 7 days to be cured enough to be placed back into service. You also have the downside of having to deal with higher VOC content and the use of solvent cleanup instead of just soap and water with water-based paints.

Oil-based paints also may have a better tendency to mildew more easily, especially in wet or humid climates. The addition of mildewcide to the paint definitely helps prevent this, but it is something to consider.

Water-based Enamels

Ever since the first water-based paint came out in the 1940s, their formulas and market share have been getting better and better. Personally, I believe their performance is close to rivaling oil-based enamels, but still not quite there.

Water-based enamels dry faster (4 hrs to re-coat) unlike their oil-based cousins and while this is great for speed of application, it often results in more brush marks and not as smooth of a finish since the paint doesn't have time to level out properly.

At the time of this writing, I have found trouble with certain very quick drying water-based paints that has a 2 hr or less redcoat time to have adhesion problems on the glass. Whichever paint you choose, make sure the manufacturer says that it is acceptable for painting onto the glass since that is the all important seal to protect your windows.

Water-based paints are also notorious for having issues with blocking. If you do end up using a water-based paint for windows and doors, make sure it is not a standard house paint but rather a specialized paint designed for windows and doors. Most paint manufacturers make a few options that are better at preventing blocking than their standard lines.

Here are some of my current favorites:
1. Sherwin Williams SherCryl (water-based)
2. Sherwin Williams Porch & Floor Enamel (water-based)
3. Benjamin Moore Impervo (oil-based)

> **PRO TIP**
>
> Add a mildewcide to any exterior paint (especially oil-based paints) for extra protection against mildew. It's cheap and easy insurance for a better paint job!

USING PRE-TREATMENTS

Using a pre-treatment to better prepare your wood sash to accept primer and paint can be a great way to extend the life of your coatings. You've got the sash down to bare wood, so now is the time to make sure you've got a sound, healthy wood that will last another hundred years or more. There are two pre-treatments that I often use to make sure my sash last and I'll discuss both of them.

Borate Pre-Treatment

Products like BoraCare or Timbor are great insurance against rot and termite damage in the future. There are a lot of different borate treatments that you can use, but these seem to be the most popular.

What a borate treatment does is add boric acid to the wood, which makes it an inhospitable place for fungus (aka rot) to grow and also make it unpalatable to termites and other wood destroying organisms. If the wood doesn't taste good, they will quickly loose interest in eating it.

Application of borates (like the two listed above) is relatively simple. You dilute them according to the manufacturer's direction and either spray or brush it onto all surfaces of the wood and then let it dry for a couple of days. Once the drying period has passed, you can begin the restoration process again.

They don't apply like a paint where you have to worry about brush marks or anything else. It's a very thin liquid like water that dries quickly and soaks into the wood.

BoraCare borate treatment

You do want to use caution when working with boric acid because, well, it has the word "acid" in the name and anything with that in the name deserves some gloves and eye protection.

Think of a borate treatment as life insurance for your windows. You don't have to have it, but it's cheap and saves you potential heartache down the line.

Old Wood Pre-Treatment

The pre-treatment that I use has been extensively tested by noted preservationist John Leeke as a consolidating oil-resin pre-treatment. He has used it for decades with great success and we have been using it for years in our shop with excellent results as well.

It serves two purposes here: 1) To rejuvenate old dried out wood and 2) To create a stronger bond between the primer and wood.

The pre-treatment soaks deep into the wood and when the primer is applied before the pre-treatment is completely dry, it creates a mechanical bond between the two, locking the primer down into the wood.

This pre-treatment is not necessary if you have healthy, fresh wood on your sash but rather is great way to prepare older, more dried out wood that is dying of thirst. When you apply it, you'll notice the older the wood the more it drinks this stuff in usually.

1. **Pre-Treatment**
   - Generously apply previously prepared pre-treatment of 3 parts Penetrol to 1 part turpentine to outside face of sash with chip brush. *(Do not apply to interior, sides, bottom of bottom sash, top of top sash or glazing rabbets.)*
   - After 5-10 minutes, wipe sash down with a clean rag to help pre-treatment apply more evenly and wipe off excess.
2. **Priming**
   - When pre-treatment is tacky to touch (approximately 15-45 mins) apply oil-based primer (NOT latex primer) with a high quality brush. Brush in thoroughly and tip off to smooth out finish.

Apply pre-treatment generously

The key with this pre-treatment is to get the timing right with your primer. You have to wait for the "tacky" feel to the surface in order to get that super mechanical bond. If it's too early or too late, it won't destroy your primer, but you won't get that extra bond we want to achieve.

CHAPTER 14
GLASS OPTIONS

What kind of glass was originally in your windows? I don't know, but there are a lot of options depending on the age of your house, your location, and how fancy your house is.

Wavy Glass

Antique, wavy glass is typically thinner than standard glass sizes today and I would definitely encourage you to save that special old glass, if at all possible. Wavy glass, depending on the age of your house, was either hand-blown for the oldest homes (pre-1850s) or machine drawn cylinder glass for the younger houses (1850s-1950s). Whichever type you have, it is priceless. They aren't making it anymore and once it's gone, it's gone forever.

These old types of glass are more brittle than the annealed glass that is available today, so be extra careful when removing and cleaning antique glass. It is easy to break if you're not careful. Antique glass is often very thin compared to today's options and may not be 100% flat.

Sometimes the old glass is broken and you need a replacement. So, with that in mind, here are some modern options to help you get the job done and maybe even eek out some energy savings.

> **PRO TIP**
>
> Always carry larger pieces of glass vertically to avoid stress and chances of breaking glass, especially thin, antique glass, which is more fragile.

Replica Glass

If you are a purist and can't stand the idea of have flat glass in your old windows, there are options for you. There are manufacturers who make replica wavy glass in stupid forms to try to match the different age buildings around the world. You can find glass to match (pretty closely, but not exactly) the old glass from the 1700s all the way up the 1940s. The older stuff has more wavy and rippled and inclusions and it slow got cleaner and smoother until the 1950 when they invented the method we still use today, which creates virtually flawless glass.

Here's a quick list of some of the companies that have historic replica glass available today.

- Hollanders Glass
- AGW Glass
- Flickinger Glassworks
- Pioneer Glass

Single Strength Annealed

Single strength glass is available at most glass suppliers. It is a mere 3/32" thick and it can be very fragile due to its thinness. I generally stay away from single strength glass unless the glazing rabbets are very thin and cannot afford a thicker glass.

One advantage single strength glass has is that it will likely not change the weight of the sash from the original glass, which means that you won't have to add to the weights for double or single-hung windows.

Double Strength Annealed

At 1/8" thick, double strength glass has been my go to glass for most projects. To replace missing or broken glass, double strength glass provides an easy to work with option that is also much harder to break than single strength. It also adds minimal extra weight to the sash which often does not need any addition of extra counter balance weights.

Tempered

Tempered glass is available in multiple thicknesses, just like regular glass, but its biggest advantage is that, when broken, it shatters into thousands of harmless little pieces that won't harm you. It is heat treated to accomplish this and the process also makes the glass harder and more default to break. Tempered glass is also called "safety glazing" and is required by code in certain windows like near showers, in doors, or in windows that are close to the floor. Installing tempered glass in these areas is a good idea if possible to keep everyone safe.

The challenge with tempered glass is that it cannot be cut. You buy tempered glass in the exact size you need and install it. If you try to cut and resize tempered glass, the whole sheet will shatter leaving you with a mess and no glass. So, double check your measurements before you order your tempered glass from the supplier.

Laminated

Laminated glass is another form of safety glazing you can get with some specific benefits. Laminated glass is essentially two pieces of standard annealed glass glued together with a very thin piece of plastic sandwiched between them. When looking through the glass, you can't tell that it is two pieces, so don't worry about appearances. It comes in a multitude of thickness for almost any application as well.

Laminated glass has two extraordinary benefits that can make it an excellent choice. Its design makes it extremely resistant to break-ins since even when the glass breaks, it is all still held together by the plastic inside. Because of this, laminated glass is extremely impact resistant.

Laminated glass is also an excellent choice for sound dampening. The thicker glass and multi piece construction helps block noise transfer and can result in a noticeably quite room where installed. This same construction and extra thickness also adds a small amount of energy efficiency over standard annealed glass.

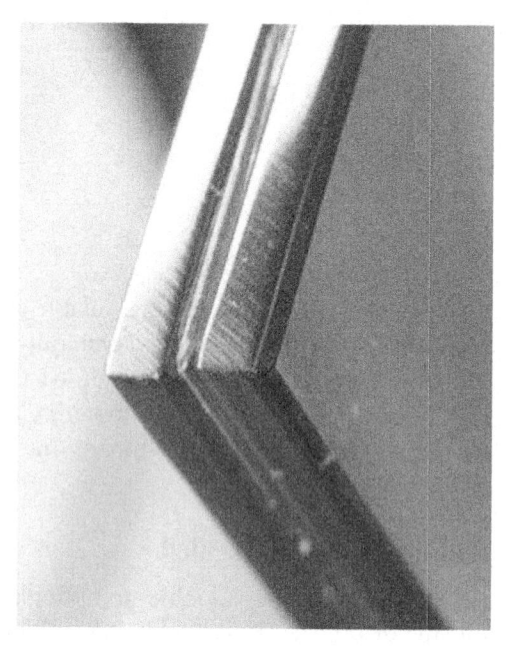

Laminated glass cross section

Low-E

There are dozens of different types of low-e coating available for glass and you can get almost any type of glass in a low-e version. Low-e stands for "low emissivity" which means, in layman's terms, that the glass reflects heat more than it allows it to pass through. Low-e glass is extremely helpful in very warm sunny climates, but maybe not as helpful in northern climates where you want the solar heat gain in the winter.

Low-e glass has so many options that it's best to discuss it with your local glass supplier to help understand which, if any, would be best for you. Adding these coating can definitely make a difference on cooling costs, but it come with a steep price tag, as low-e glass is one of the most expensive options you can get.

Insulated Glass Units (IGU)

Today, most new windows are manufactured with double-paned glass, otherwise called IGUs. The industry claims the energy saving benefits of insulated glass, which is a terrible oxymoron since glass is itself not an insulating material, but the science is a little fuzzy in my opinion.

Does an IGU do a better job of blocking heat and cold from transferring through a window than the same window with simple single-paned glass? Yes. Does that equal a savings to the homeowner? Not exactly, and here's why. Almost any IGU that you buy from a manufacturer comes with a 10 year warranty. That doesn't mean that it will fog up and fail at 10 years and 1 day, but it means the manufacturer wouldn't be surprised if it did.

Having to pay for the materials and labor of glass replacement on your windows every 10 years can add up and eliminate the small savings in energy costs you may be getting. In my opinion, it's not a good idea and it rarely makes a dent big enough in energy costs to justify the added materials in the landfill and headache they inevitably cause.

Insulated Glass Unit (IGU)

Bowed Glass

Some windows installed on curved portions of buildings like turrets are fortunate enough to have bowed glass in their bowed sashes. This glass is a little harder to find and work with, but it can be very satisfying when restored, due to the uniqueness of this glass.

Companies like Flickinger's can make and ship bowed glass cut to size right to you. I don't recommend trying to cut this glass for the average homeowner as it can be fraught with challenges. It's best to get a precise measurement and order the right size. Leave cutting bowed glass to the pros.

Plate Glass

This is another thicker form of antique glass that was the cat's meow back in the day. Plate glass is almost always much thicker (sometimes 1/4" or more) than wavy glass and has less imperfections. It was polished in the factory to remove those imperfections and smooth out the surface.

It really functions much the same way as regular wavy glass in that it can be cut on site. It does make the sash much heavier due to its thickness, and was often used in prominent homes or windows since it was terribly expensive.

CHAPTER 15
STORMS & SCREENS

I live in Florida and until I began traveling north, the only thing I knew of a storm window was from the houses on the coast that had big aluminum rollers over their windows that were closed during the hurricanes.

Traditional wood screens and storms are very much the same thing in an old house, other than the obvious differences. They are both built with an almost identical wood frame that hangs on the same hardware so that they could be easily interchanged, depending on the season. I saw easily, but anyone who has ever tried to climb a ladder and take a 30 lbs. storm down from the second story of their houses knows that each time you get safely to the ground again, you feel like you've cheated death.

Today, there are options for installing storm windows other than the traditional wood exterior storms, like interior storms or exterior aluminum operable storms. For modern exterior storms, there are plenty of manufacturers around that you can look into. Below is a list of a just a few companies that I trust to make attractive and high-quality exterior storm windows:

- Monray
- Allied Window
- SpencerWorks
- Custom Built

EXTERIOR STORMS

Exterior storm windows are a uniquely northern solution to keep houses warm during the cold winters. Traditional wood storms are a very simple and long lasting option, but there are also modern aluminum options on the market that can make a big difference as well.

If your house doesn't have exterior storms and you live in a primarily hot climate, then you should skip down to the section on interior storms, but for the rest of the country, this section can be a major money saver.

Traditional wood storm window *Aluminum storm window*

    Wood storms are built much the same way as wood sash. They can rot and should be repaired with either a dutchman or epoxy, like detailed in Part I. They are usually glazed with the same glazing putties and painted with the same exterior paints. They should fit snuggly in the opening and work best when weatherstripped properly.

    Too often, the weatherstripping is poorly done or missing/damaged and this can cause big problems. Missing weatherstripping just results in less efficiency, but overzealous attempts to completely seal the storm window inevitably cause moisture and rot issues for both the storm and primary window. There should always be weep holes at the top and bottom of the storms to allow a small amount of air exchange so that the moisture that gets between the storm and the primary window can evaporate and escape. I can't stress the importance of these weeps holes enough.

    For after market storm windows, this isn't much of an issues since all of the manufacturers that I know of provide the weep holes into their designs. Traditional wood storms are, in my opinion, more attractive than the after market aluminum options, but there is something to be said for the simple convenience of operable storm windows that you don't have to remove every season.

Whichever way you decide to go, an exterior storm window provides extraordinary protection from the elements to your primary window and will save you considerably on energy bills.

Interior Storms

Interior storm panels are a relatively new offering to help homeowners with a host of window issues like:
- Air-Sealing
- Condensation
- Noise Abatement
- Privacy
- Heat-Blocking

Interior storm panel

These panels are typically measured to fit very specifically on the inside of your existing window with little to no modification. Their primary function is air-sealing, which they can do an excellent job of if they are measured and installed properly. They can cut air infiltration down to minuscule levels better than even the most high end energy efficient window available today.

This air sealing can be coupled with other features like sound blocking of up to 70%, UV blocking coatings that reduce heat transfer, privacy glazing, or even black out versions for night shift workers.

There are also homemade versions of these panels that DIYers can make themselves that work nearly as good as the after market models if you can get the tight seal, which is the trick to their energy efficiency gains.

There are several companies that make these interior storms today and below are just a few of the most popular.

- Indow
- Innerglass

Old Windows In-Depth

- Magnetite

Making Affordable Screens

Once you've got your old windows working again, it's time to get some screens. A lot of people don't think about this until after we restore their windows and they are anxious to open them, but don't want to fight the bugs.

You can get cheap screens made at any hardware store, but why would you want to obscure those beautifully restored window windows with a cheap bargain screen?

Traditionally, on these old windows, you would have found wood screens that complimented their appearance. Many of those screens have been tucked away in the attic or basement, so taking a peak there first might yield results, but most slowly fell apart and ended up in the landfill.

In the early 20th century, these screens were not particularly well made. They were usually held together by corrugated metal fasteners and screened with galvanized steel, or in higher end applications, bronze screening.

There are some houses that had very nice mortise and tenon screens, but that seems to be the exception rather than the rule, in my experience. For years, my company would only make the mortise and tenon style until I realized that there had to be a more affordable option. Nobody would buy these high end screens because, after all, it was only a screen and mortise and tenon joinery makes things expensive.

So, we studied how the old ones were made and started making them just the same way. The result is a much more affordable and very doable screen for the average DIYer to make. In this chapter I'll show you how we do it.

Corrugated fasteners

Step 1 Determine the Thickness

Screens were meant to fit on the outside of a double hung window and rest up against the blind stop. They are usually between 3/4" and 1 1/8" thick. The 3/4" version is extremely simple since you can just buy standard 1x4 and 1x6 materials to make the screens from.

For thicker screens, you have 3 options:
1. Use a thicker stock to accommodate the size you need
2. Fur out the blind stop a bit so as to leave 3/4" of an inch remaining
3. Ad furring strips to the perimeter of your 3/4" screen to accommodate the thickness

Step 2 Measure the Opening

The next thing you need to measure are the overall dimensions of the screen (width & height). I measure as tight as possible and then subtract an 1/8" from the overall size. If you make the screens too tight, then with the irregularities and paint build up on old windows, you will be doing a lot of planing and sanding to make it fit. If you measure and come up with 32" x 60" then plan to make your screens 31 7/8" x 59 7/8" to ensure a good fit.

Step 3 Cut to Length

You'll need (1) 1x4 cut to the height of your window (the 59 7/8" length from our previous example) and (1) 1x6 cut to the width of the window (32") minus 3 1/2". *There is reason for the slight discrepancy and it has to do with the blade width on the table saw. For now, just trust that the rule is correct. You'll see why soon!*

You'll also need enough screen molding to go around the perimeter of the screen and across the meeting rail of your screen. So, for a 32"x60" screen, you'd need approximately 18'. Screen molding or half round is available at most home stores and that's what you'll use to give the screens their finished appearance.

Step 4 Rip the Rails

From these 2 pieces of wood, you'll be able to make all the rails and stiles you need for one full screen. You'll need the table saw for this next part to rip these pieces to the proper width. Here is the cut list you need:
- 1x4: 2 pieces @ 1 11/16" each. *Accommodating for the width of the blade this should be cutting the 1x4 exactly down the center so you have two identical width boards.*
- 1x6: 1 piece @ 1 11/16", 1 piece at 1", and remainder should be about 2 9/16"

Step 5 Assemble

Assemble the screen frame and clamp everything together so that it is square. Then nail each joint with either a pneumatic corrugated fastener gun or hand nail each joint with the corrugated fasteners using a corrugated nail set. Hand nailing these fasteners is not always easy. Even with the nail set, you will have fasteners crumple or not set properly on occasion. I will say that if you are only building one or two screens, the nail set will work, but the pneumatic gun makes the job immensely easier, especially for larger jobs.

You'll need two fasteners in each joint except for the meeting rail, which only gets one. For extra stability, you also add some waterproof wood glue like Titebond III to each joint.

You can also use a pocket hole jig and screws to attach the joints if you are more familiar and comfortable with that method.

Step 6 Prime & Paint

It's much easier to prime and paint screens before you apply the screening, so take this time to put a coat of oil-based primer on and coat the frame and screen molding with a high quality paint.

Step 7 Apply Screening

Pick the screen type you want and roll it out across the frame. Start in a corner and begin pulling and stapling the screening tight. You want to staple with the first 1/2" from the inside edge of the frame in order to hide the staples in the end.

Step 8 Apply Screen Molding

Cut pieces of screen mold to cover the areas stapled earlier and nail it on with 3/4" 18 ga. nails. Miter the corners for an attractive finish.

Step 9 Install Hardware

Touch up the paint on any nails holes and then apply the screen hardware. You may still have old screen hangers on your window trim, but you need the female portion that goes on the screen itself. You also need to have a simple hook and eye to attach the bottom of the screen into place and secure it.

Step #4 Rip rails

Step #5 Assemble parts

Step #5 Nail joints

Step #8 Apply screening

Step #9 Install hardware

Old Windows In-Depth

CHAPTER 16
PUTTY OPTIONS

Putty, putty as far as the eye can see. Putty, putty, which should I choose for me? There are a bunch of options out there for glazing putty, some of which are good and some of which are a waste of time.

I'll give you the run down on some of the most popular and widely available putties, as well as a few speciality putties for those special circumstances.

Sarco MultiGlaze

For the professional window restorers I know, this is by far the most popular putty. Just like Trident, 4 out of 5 restorers seem to use it and I understand why. For glazing windows in a shop, it is easy to use and cures quickly so that the sash already for paint in just a few days, rather than a couple weeks for most putties.

Easy to work and affordable- you really can't beat this putty. It is for shop use only and must be painted before being set outside, which is really its only problem, otherwise I doubt I'd use any other putty.

Sarco DualGlaze

DualGlaze is Sarco's solution to needing to glaze outdoors on wood or steel windows. It is a slower curing, taking about 2-3 weeks before being ready for paint. It remains more flexible than other putties, which prolongs its service life.

It does tend to be a bit oilier than MultiGlaze and is not as smooth to tool, but the differences can be fixed by the addition of some extra whiting to the mix.

Sarco DualGlaze

DAP 33

About the only thing DAP 33 has going for it is that it can be found in almost any hardware and paint store in America. DAP seems to have put their focus on marketing rather than product development when it comes to DAP 33.

The putty is bright white, which does make it easy to cover when painting white sash, but it difficult to tool and messy to work with. Also, after a few years of service, it becomes extremely chalky and doesn't seem to respond to steam heat for removal, which makes that much more angry with it.

DAP 1012

1012 is DAP's putty designed for use on steel and aluminum windows. It doesn't feel much different from DAP 33 to work with, but DAP says the formulation is designed specifically for metal windows rather than wood.

Crawford's Putty

This putty showed up at my local paint store one day so I thought I'd give it a try. I have to say, I don't have a lot of experience with it, but I was pleasantly surprised by how workable and easy to glaze it was. The application process was very similar to Sarco MultiGlaze and left a nice finished product.

Glazol

This is a fairly nondescript putty to me. It is white like DAP 33, Glazes relatively easy, though not notably great, has an average drying time of about a week. It kind of strides the line between all of the putties that I mentioned above and is neither hot nor cold to me.

I mention it because while I may not be a huge fan, it may really be a great glazing putty for someone who appreciates its

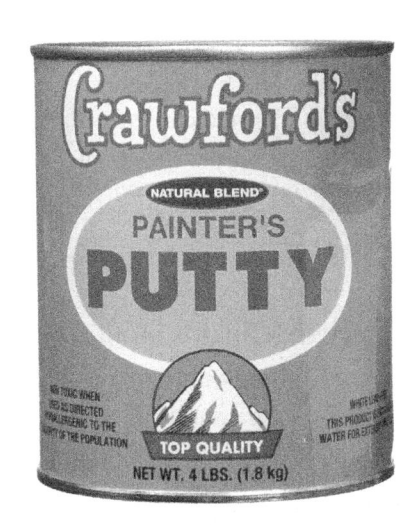

Dap '33'

Crawford's putty

Old Windows In-Depth

characteristics. Different strokes for different folks, and this one might be yours.

Allback

For the purist, this is your putty. It is pure whiting and linseed oil just like great-great-grandpa used to make. This is traditional linseed oil putty. It is pretty decent to work with, though a little messier than I would prefer.

The big advantage to this stuff is that if you are using Allback's linseed oil paint, you can paint the moment after you glaze. No waiting for a skin to develop on the putty! That's a big convenience and time savings.

Allback

AquaGlaze

This is a totally different kind of putty from the others so far. It is an acrylic glazing compound as opposed to oil-based. It also dries extremely quickly, like just a few hours instead of days before it's ready for paint.

That makes AquaGlaze a great option for quick glass replacements onsite. Also, since it is acrylic and not oil-based, it doesn't have the same potential for mildew issues. I have seen some long term testing showing that it does not stay flexible for long, so I try to save this one for emergencies only.

Sherwin Williams "66" Glazing Compound

I've seen this putty on the shelf at my local Sherwin Williams store and have wondered how it performed, so I forked over a few bucks and brought a quart back to the shop for testing.

AquaGlaze

The putty is white in appearance just like DAP 33 and when I dug it out of the container, I found it to be a sticky, gooey mess to work with. It stuck to everything, including my gloves- so much so, that I had to take them off and use my bare hands.

The stickiness of the putty made it feel more like a paste than a knife grade putty. The stickiness did make it easy to adhere to the glazing rabbet, but other than that, I did not enjoy working with this putty one bit. Trying to tool a smooth finish was not an easy task, and I'm a pretty darn good glazier.

Cure time was about 13 days before it was ready for painting. Even if this putty performs amazingly, I would not recommend it because it was such a pain to work with.

Chapter 17
Advanced Sash Repair

Dutchman repairs in depth

A Dutchman repair is one of the most useful repairs a good carpenter can learn. It can take some practice to and trial and error before your Dutchmans are able to blend seamlessly, but it can be done and when done properly, a good dutchman will last a long time.

I actually worked with a Dutch carpenter once and he was baffled why I called it a dutchman. I explained it to him and he said they just called that a "patch" which made sense, I guess. Dutch carpenters used to patch wood more than fully rebuild things like other carpenters, I guess. At the time, it was a dig against them but to me, it seems more like an efficient use of material.

The basic premise is to remove a section of damaged or missing wood and replace it with new, healthy wood. There are a couple of considerations before starting a repair that you need to have worked out.

> **PRO TIP**
>
> When possible, use the same species of wood and try to have the grain run the same direction for a Dutchman repair for the best performance.

First, match the wood species and grain direction as closely as possible. If you patch Eastern white pine with mahogany, which is a very different wood, you won't have good results, because these wood species behave very differently.

Each species of wood expands and contracts differently from others and having a patch that will shrink and swell similarly to the original wood will keep the patch from eventually being pushed out by the old wood.

Just like each species is different, the grain orientation makes a difference as well. Be careful to keep the grain all running the same direction. If you install your patch with the grain running perpendicular to the old wood, then it will expand and contract in different ways, causing early failure again.

Step 1 Mark Your Repair

Begin by marking a square or rectangular section around the damaged wood. You want to cut out a simple shape that can easily patched. If you cut a jagged and odd shaped patch, then cutting a mating piece to replace it will make things that much more difficult. Make sure to mark beyond where the rot or damage is so that you will be cutting into healthy wood.

Step 2 Cut the Damaged Section Out

Using whatever tool is most appropriate, cut your patch out. Small repairs are usually best done with a hand saw, chisel, or multi-tool, while larger repairs may be best on a table saw or circular saw. It just depends on what you are most comfortable using.

Step 3 Prepare Your Patch

Find a piece of similar species knot free wood and line up the grain, like we discussed earlier. One more consideration is to make sure your patch is slightly thicker than the object you are patching. For example, most window sash are 1 3/8" so a patch that is 1 1/2" or even 1 3/4" thick is a great choice so that you can sand it completely level later. Cut the patch so that it has a nice tight fit with no gaps and runs a little long, wide, and thick where it can to allow plenty of material to sand off later. Dry fit and make sure it is exactly how you want it.

Step 4 Glue Up

Once you've got the perfect patch, apply a waterproof wood glue like Titebond III liberally to the mating surfaces and clamp, nail, or screw the patch in place making sure you get some glue squeeze out which proves you have good contact. Smaller patches can be clamped, but larger pieces may need a couple of 18 ga nails to help it stay in place and even

Dutchman ready for filling and sanding

larger patches may require screws or dowels to hold it in place, but this is rare since proper gluing and clamping is usually sufficient.

Step 5 Fill & Sand

Once the glue has setup for about 24 hrs, pull the clamps off and fill in any small gaps with wood filler or epoxy and then sand everything smooth and level.

A good Dutchman is a big time and money saver for damaged window sash. It is usually best for only patching surfaces because, just like any patch on a stained varnished surface, you will notice the patch, but on painted sash, this repair can completely disappear, and that's ultimately what we want.

GLAZING BAR REPAIRS

One of the more delicate pieces of a window sash are the glazing bars. A lot of people call these different names, but we all spend hours repairing them virtually the same way.

For small repairs, epoxy can work well, but these delicate pieces are often better repaired with this straight forward technique that is really just a modified dutchman repair.

The two tools I use here are a small Japanese saw and a sharp chisel. You'll also need some wood glue and painter's tape.

Step 1 Cut End Notches

Using your hand saw, cut an angled notch at either end of the section you wish to repair all the way down to the bottom of the glazing rabbet. If you recall your geometry, you will be cutting out a trapezoid shaped piece.

Step 2 Remove Damaged Section

Using that sharp chisel, carefully work the section you cut out free from the sash. Chiseling along the grain of the wood will allow you to slowly get down until the damaged section is completely flush with the glazing rabbet. You can finish it off with a small piece of sandpaper if necessary.

Step 3 Cut Replacements

Cut a piece of wood to match the shape of the void you just made. Just like with the Dutchman, make it slightly larger and wider than the original glazing bar so that it can be sanded later.

Step 4 Glue & Tape

Apply a waterproof wood glue like Titebond III to the glazing rabbet and patch and then slide it into place. It should fit snugly and securely. One you have it right where you want it, wrap some painter's tape around the muntin to hold it in place until the glue has dried.

Step 5 Sand & Finish

After 24 hrs, take the tape off and sand, plane, or chisel down any high spots. Once it's all leveled out, you're good to go.

4. Glue in replacement glazing bar

5. Level out repair

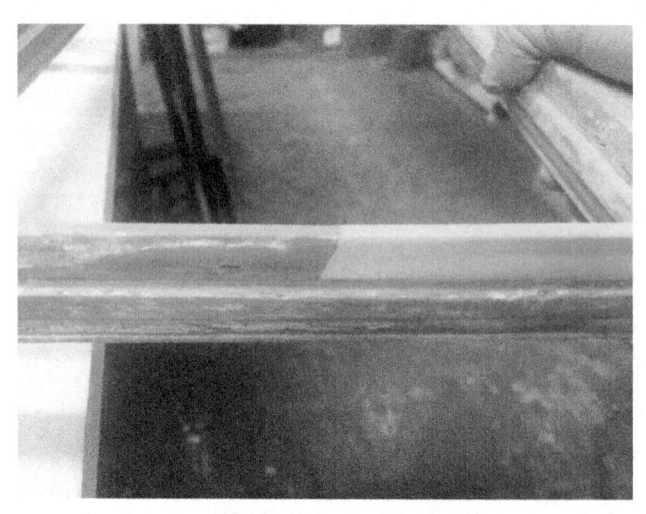

Completed glazing bar dutchman

Old Windows In-Depth

Joinery Repairs

The joints of old wood windows are often prone to decay because they are a good place for water to get trapped and wreak havoc. Understanding how to repair and stabilize these joints is imperative if they are damaged.

When the glass is removed from a wood sash, there is some racking that can be expected. Don't expect a bare sash to be completely sturdy. Some flexibility in the frame is acceptable as long as it doesn't feel wobbly or loose. The reinstallation of the glass will help stabilize the frame. It's the very loose or rotted joints that we want to focus on in this chapter.

Repairing Loose Joints

Old sash joints can loosen up over time and sometimes make the sash a little too wobbly. Fortunately, this is a rather simple repair. The important part is getting the sash square before securing the joints again.

Set your sash on a stable work surface, and using a framing square, make sure the sash is completely square and clamp it into place. Once your sash is square, it's just a matter of pinning the joints in place, which there are two options for doing.

The simplest way is to shoot two 15 ga. 1 1/4" nails into the joints, making sure you go through the tenon inside. I prefer nailing on the interior of the sash to prevent water from possibly affecting the nails, causing rust later, and then setting the nails behind the surface of the wood and filling the nail holes. Stainless steel nails are a nice upgrade to make a lasting repair.

The other option if you want to avoid using nails is to drill a 1/4" hole through the joint (again in two places for stability) and insert 1/4" dowels into the holes. This repair is more appropriate for sash built before 1900, which is when joints were more likely to be pegged rather than nailed.

Repairing Rotten Joints

If you have rot damage to a joint, then resolving this is imperative. The rot will continue if left untreated and can quickly disintegrate a sash, causing glass to fall out or other catastrophic damage that is much harder to fix.

Step 1 Remove Damaged Wood

Any loose or irreparably damaged wood should be removed with an awl or chisel until you get back to solid wood again. You should be better able to asses the full extent of the damage at this point.

Step 2 Apply Borate Treatment

We spoke about it in Chapter 9, but a borate treatment is absolutely necessary in this case. It will kill the fungus, causing the rot and make sure it does not come back. Apply the treatment liberally and let it dry to the manufacturer's specs.

Step 3 Epoxy or Dutchman?

Depending on the severity of the repair, you may either need to patch with epoxy or perform a dutchman repair first. If you're not missing large sections of the joint and only a portion of wood is damaged, then after the borate treatment, apply an epoxy consolidant like Abatron LiquidWood and then fill the missing sections with an epoxy filler like Abatron WoodEpox, making sure to overfill the repair so that it can be sanded level later.

If you are left with a joint that is completely gone, then a dutchman repair will be required.

Moderate joint repair with epoxy

If you are a skilled woodworker, then replicating the damaged portion of wood is a good option, and then splice it into the existing rail or stile. Even though the joints were not originally glued, I recommend using a waterproof wood glue when replacing whole portions of a joint. If you feel confident enough to replicate portions of the rail or stile, I shouldn't need to give you much guidance for attaching what you build.

Epoxy Option

If you aren't a skilled woodworker, then an epoxy repair may be your best bet. For this repair, I use dowels to reattach the two pieces of the joint and keep them in proper alignment while the rest of the joint is rebuilt with epoxy. Many epoxies are structural epoxies and can handle the stresses of a wood window joint as long as they have a frame work to attach to.

Step 1 Square & Drill

Set your sash on a solid work surface and clamp it into proper alignment so that the frame is completely square and level. You may have to get creative with your clamps since it is missing a corner joint. Next, drill through the rail into the stile (or stile into the rail) with a 1/2" drill bit in two locations. This will allow you to insert 2 dowels which work better than just one for keeping the window square. Make sure that you drill at least a couple of inches into solid, sound wood.

Step 2 Glue & Dowel

Clean out the holes that you drilled with a vacuum and apply waterproof wood glue liberally to a couple lengths of 1/2" dowels and carefully insert them into the holes that you just drilled. It's easiest to leave them plenty long and trim the excess later. Take this moment to make sure the sash is still square and everything is tight. Let it cure.

Step 3 Epoxy the Gaps

Once the glue is dry (usually 24 hrs) remove the clamps and pick up what should be a stable sash. Using the dowels as a skeleton for your epoxy repairs, you can now fill in the missing wood sections with epoxy filler. Make sure to overfill the repair and then carve and sand the repair to match any missing profiles.

CHAPTER 18
WORKING WITH STEAM

Steam is a powerful tool when it comes to window restoration. It helps you work safely and dust free and you can use it for any number of chores. It is a whiz at softening old glazing putty, which can help you save that old wavy glass. It softens and loosen layers of paint to remove it from flats and profiles alike.

It's no secret that heat helps to remove old paint and putty, but steam brings a safer alternative since it virtually eliminates the risk of fire and also minimizes the lead risks because you are working with wet paint that keeps dust at a minimum.

For those reasons, it's something to consider if you are restoring more than just a couple of windows. It definitely speeds up the process.

One of the concerns people often mention when working with steam is if it will adversely affect the moisture content of the wood. From experience, I can tell you that the moisture content of the wood is raised marginally for a matter of hours, and then quickly returns to normal.

My homemade steam box

I have also never experienced a sash bowing or warping from the steaming process. The only adverse affect I ave experienced is that it does make the wood softer for a couple of hours until it can return to its normal moisture content, so you have to be careful to not gouge the wood when scraping.

Deglazing with Steam

Almost every sash we deglaze is done after a time in our steam box. I find that we can save a ton more old glass and it shortens the deglazing process, so it's worth its weight in gold. There is nothing that speeds up putty removal faster and better than steam, and with such a low cost to buy a steamer and build on of these boxes, it makes it well worth the investment if you plan to do multiple windows. With steam, we can deglaze a 6-lite sash in about 15-20 mins vs. 1 hr. or more without steam.

I recommend a commercial garment steamer like a Jiffy J-4000 to power your steam box. A cheap home version won't produce enough steam for anything other than doing spot work. You need something with some heft to keep that steam box filled to the brim so that the sashes get hot and stay hot for awhile.

Here are the basic steps for deglazing with steam:

1. Place sash in steam box until putty is softened (usually 1 hr.)
2. When removing sash from steam box, open door and wait a minimum of 15 seconds for temperature to regulate. Failure to do so may result in broken glass.
3. Take sash to work table putty side up and close steam box door.
4. Using a firm 2" or 3" putty knife or 5-in-1 tool, remove putty by sliding putty knife underneath putty along glass surface. Do not run knife between wood and putty as this may gouge the soft wood. If putty is still stubborn, it may require more time in the steam box.
5. Once all putty has been removed, remove metal glazing points using a chisel or sharp putty knife to pry them out or pull them out using needle nose pliers. Gently catch the end of the glazing point with the chisel and working carefully attempt to slide it out of the wood rabbet.
6. Double check to ensure all glazing points are out.
7. Using a Sharpie, label glass with sash number. If there are more than one pane of glass label them top left to bottom right as you would read a book with the sash number followed by the pane number (ie. 12-1, 12-2, etc.) Gently remove glass and set aside.

If you don't plan on using steam, then the process is a bit more tedious, but much the same. You'll need to chip out all the existing putty from the exterior of the sash. Use a chisel, putty knife, razor knife or any other tool that you find effective. Be careful through this process to not gouge the wood.

You can find plans to build your own steam cabinet for about $200 in materials at various places online.

REMOVING PAINT WITH STEAM

Paint removal is always a bear, but steam can make it a bit easier. The moist heat causes the paint to lose its bond with the wood and start to bubble and peel away.

The softness is not long lasting, so you have to work quickly and in small sections. Even a basic garment steamer can work great for spot paint removal. Below, I've put together a few tips for removing paint with steam.

Keep it Close

Keep the steam source close the paint surface. If not, the steam heat will quickly dissipate and not penetrate the paint layers, rendering the steam relatively ineffective.

Keep it Small

Work in small 2-3 inch sections to keep the paint hot. Once it starts to bubble or soften, scrape that area while you move the steamer to the next section.

Pull Scrapers Only

Since you're using steam, the wood will be softening up and that makes it all to easy to gouge or damage the surface with a push scraper. Use a sharp pull style scraper to gently remove the paint from the surface.

Sand Later

After the wood has had time to dry out (usually a couple hours) come back and give the surface a light sanding. If you were successful, there should't be too much sanding work for you later.

CHAPTER 19
UNIQUE MECHANICALS

SPIRAL BALANCES

While most of the windows on historic buildings built before WWII used the simple and effective rope and pulley counterweight system, there are some that utilize different balances systems. A popular option were spiral balances, sometimes called a tube balance because when it installed, it looks like a tube on the jamb.

These balances are not terribly complicated, but they can be troublesome to work with if you're not familiar with them. I'll be speaking specifically about one of the more common types I've come across, but there are dozens of variations made by several manufacturers.

The advantages of these balances is that they are a relatively simple design and can be tensioned to meet the weight of the sash in question. There are different size balances to meet the needs of differing height sashes.
They also eliminate the need for weight pockets and can be installed in smaller rough openings and allow for larger window sizes.

The problem with them is that, just like any delicate mechanical item, they can rust, dent, bend or otherwise break rendering them unworkable, and in a lot of cases, they are not repairable unless you can salvage missing/broken parts from a similar balance.

How To Remove Spiral Balances

This style balance is held in place with a single screw at the top corner of the jamb and one or 2 screws on the bottom of the sash. Each sash requires 2 balances (one on each side) to support it properly.

Before removing the balance, you have to know that it is under tension and when the screws are removed, the balance will spin dramatically to remove the tension. Depending on the weight of the sash, this tension may be significant, so do be careful when removing them.

Step 1 Remove Top Screw

On the bottom sash, remove the screw in the top corner of the jamb, holding the tube in place. These screws are notoriously difficult to remove, since they have been in place for decades with tons of caked on paint or corrosion.

If the screws are so stubborn that they simply won't move (which is often the case) I usually end up wedging a pry-bar behind the tube and giving them a few swift pops to pry the screw out. These screws are more like a spiral shank nail than anything, so they come out easier than a typical screw would when pried out.

Step 2 Remove the Support Bracket

After the retaining screw at the top is removed, there is only one other place that needs to be removed to get the balance off, and that is the screws in the bracket underneath the sash.

For a top sash this is underneath the meeting rail on either side of the sash. For a bottom sash, it is on the bottom rail that rests on the sill when closed.

There will be one or two screws holding the bracket in place depending on the style of balance. You don't need to remove the bottom bracket in order to remove the sash from the jamb, but to do any work on the sash or balance, you will have to remove it, so it's best done now.

Remember, these balances are under tension and will spin like the dickens when the first screw is removed, so be careful. Now, let's look at repair and reinstallation.

How To Repair Spiral Balances

I keep a stock of these in my shop because you

Remove top screw

Remove support bracket

never know when you're going to need spare parts and the parts are not simple to find always. A salvage yard is a good place to find replacements if you need them, or you can try manufacturers like Caldwell and Swisco who still make versions of this balance.

Fixing Bent Balances

Most of the repairs I do with spiral balances are to straighten out bent balances. This is technically easy, but can be painstaking work to get right. Spiral balances will not work properly with kinks or bends in the tube or the spiral, so straightening them out is essential to good operation.

You can use any number of tools to work out the kinks, but my favorite are a small hammer and some pliers. Bottom line: do whatever it takes to get a straight balance again.

Replacing Brackets

The brackets at the bottom often rust away or break from abuse. They can be replaced if you can find some extra junker balances to scrounge parts from.

There is a single rivet holding the bracket on in most cases that should be punched out with an awl and then you can attach a replacement bracket or have a machine shop make one for you if you can't find one to match.

Tune Up & Cleaning

The standard treatment I give all of the balances that we get in the shop is to strip all of the paint off of them with a wire wheel or steel wool and then wipe the dirty old grease from the spirals with WD40 until everything is clean and working smoothly.

How To Install Spiral Balances

This is the part that can give some folks trouble. This is the smoothest way I have found to reinstall these. I'm not proclaiming that this is the best way or the industry standard (there isn't one), but this is how I like to do it.

To start with, this whole thing can be done with just one person, but it helps a TON to have a helper to hold the sash in place while you work. If you don't have a helper, then you'll need to cut a block of wood to prop under the sash while you work to hold it in place.

Also, the steps are the same for the top sash and bottom sash, so, I'll just walk through them once and you can handle it from there.

Step 1 Set the Sash in Place

When your sash is ready to go back in and the jamb has the parting beads removed, set the top sash in its track and let it rest on the sill. Test it to make sure it slides smoothly in the jamb all the way to the top and bottom with no trouble before doing anything else.

Before setting the bottom sash, make sure the top sash is in place, working smoothly and the parting beads are all installed.

Step 2 Drop in the Balance

The next steps will all be repeated on both sides of the sash since there are two balances per sash. With the sash in place,, drop the balance, bracket end first down into the mortise on the side of the sash. It should slide all the way down to rest on the sill while you hold the top of the tube above the sash.

Tension the balance

Step 3 Attach the Tube

Pull the tube all the way up to the top of the jamb letting the spiral fall down into the sash mortise. Keep the seam on the tube toward the jamb so that it doesn't show. Attach the tube with one 1 1/2" wood screw. A pan head screw works best, but really, any attractive screw will work, since it will be visible.

There are two things that you need to focus on here:
1. Don't tighten the screw too much that you dent or flatten the tube.
2. It's imperative that you keep the tube centered in the track so that the sash can move fully up and down without binding.

Step 4 Tension the Balance

With the tube securely attached at the top, slide the sash up to the upper most position and hold it there while you tension.

Grasp the bracket, as it should have fallen through the bottom of the mortise on the side of the sash, and begin to spin it clockwise.

It will get shorter as you make the revolutions. Continue turning until the bracket is almost at the bottom of the tube and then pull it down about 6-8 inches and continue turning (adding tension) until it makes its way back to the tube again.

At this point, you should have enough tension to support a standard sash. Without letting go of the bracket, move on to the next step to attach it.

Step 5 Set Bracket

Some brackets have a little nub on the end that allows it to be lightly hammered into a small mortise on the bottom of the sash. This allows the bracket to stay in place while you get a 1″ wood screw to securely attach the bracket onto the bottom of the sash.

Some brackets may accept two screws and I prefer these, so, if there is any way to add a second screw, do it. The extra insurance is well worth it!

Set bracket then screw in place

Once both balances are attached, test the sash, moving it all the way up and down in the jamb. Stop at various points and make sure that the tension is adequate to support the sash wherever it may need to rest along its track.

You can always remove the bracket and adjust the tension (add a little, remove a little) as needed. Once you figure out the tension needed for the first window, the rest will be very similar if they're the same size.

TAPE BALANCES

In tight spots when there isn't a lot of room, the use of a tape balance is often a good choice. Tape balances have been around since the 1880s, and are still being made by some of the same companies like Caldwell, Pullman, and ACME.

A tape balance works like a modern tape measure and the advantage is that, like spiral balances and jamb liners, they don't require a weight pocket, so you can install them in tight quarters or expand what would otherwise be a small window.

Old Windows In-Depth

The other advantage is that they are pretty friendly for the average DIYer. I'll walk through the basics of working with tape balances below.

How to Size Tape Balances

If you need replacement tapes or are thinking of installing some fresh, then you have to be sure you order the right size. Tape balances are sized according to the weight that they can carry. You'll need to remove your sash from the jamb and weigh it first to determine the proper size balance. You can use a luggage scale or standard scale if you prefer.

If you have a 12 lbs. sash, then you'll need a 6 lbs. tape balance since there are two balances (one on each side). Make sense? Most of the balances come in 2 lbs. increments, which makes it simple to discern, but what do you do about odd weight sash? If you have a 14 lbs. sash that falls right in the gaps. In that case, you'd go with the next size up. You can usually round up, which is safer than going to the size below what you need.

Pullman brand tape balances

Each manufacturer has their own methods for sizing, so make sure you know what you are ordering because too strong of a balance will result in the window constantly being driven upwards, and too weak a balance will leave you with a sagging sash.

How To Install Tape Balances

If you've got existing balances, it's as easy as removing the sash and swapping out the broken balance for the new one. If you have a different balance system before and you are switching to tape balances, then it will take a little modification, depending on the current conditions of your window. I'll assume you have a rope and pulley system and are switching to tapes for this example, but the process is much the same no matter what you have.

Step 1 Mark a Template

If there is no hole, cut into the jamb already or if the opening is too small for the new tape balance, then you'll have to mark the jamb about 3-6" down from the top on each side where the tape will be mortised into the jamb.

Step 2 Mortise & Install Balance

Drill out the hole using a spade or forstner bit large enough that the body of the tape balance can fit into the mortise. The section behind the face of the balance, which has the screw holes, should also be chiseled back so that it can rest flush with the surface of the jamb just like a normal pulley.

Once you have a good fit, install the balance securely with two screws and test the operation. Never let the tape slam quickly back into the body, as this may damage the balance. Always control the tape slowly back into the balance.

Step 3 Install Tape Hook

The tape hook is the piece of the hardware that allows the balance to attach to the sash. You may have to chisel out the side of the sash a little to accommodate the tape hook before installing. Attach it (screw hole at the bottom) in the deeper part of the groove of the sash. The bottom angle piece is bent so that it will come exactly flush with the edge of the sash. If no groove exists on your sash, then notch an opening on the sash approximately 10 inches down from the top of the meeting rail.

Installed tape hook

Step 4 Attach & Install Sash

Pull the tapes down and attach them to the tape hook on each side, much like attaching ropes, and then place the sash back into the jamb. Be careful not to twist or bend the tape metal tapes as they can kink and cause problems later if you aren't careful. Test the operation and balance and then attach the parting beads and stops as detailed in Part I of this book.

Replacement Parts and Tips

There are still several companies that make tape balances today, and probably the easiest place to find them is online at Kilian's Hardware and any of the three major manufacturers that I listed above. While tape balances can occasionally be repaired when small pieces break, it usually makes sense to simply replace the broken tape with a new matching one from the same manufacturer.

Vinyl Jamb Liners

Vinyl jamb liners were sometimes installed as original balance systems and some are the result of modifications made to "modernize" old windows. When it comes to jamb liners, there are two kinds (vinyl and metal) and the ones I find most frequently used are the vinyl kind that were popular in 80s and 90s.

Of these vinyl jamb liners, there are also many versions an brands. While it's not feasible to go through the intricacies of each type, they are all very similar, and learning to work with one will help you to work with others with only slight modifications.

Most of the time these jamb liners are installed with only a single nail at the top (if that) or just some caulk at the sill. So, they can be removed fairly easily along with the sash. There are some versions that allow the sash to be tilted inward and removed that way, but those are simple enough that I decided to focus this section on the non-tilt jamb liners, since those are more problematic.

In order to properly remove one or both of the sash installed with a jamb liner, you usually it is usually best to remove the jamb liner along with the sash, so that's what I outline below.

Step 1 Remove the Stops

First, you'll want to pry off the interior stop on both sides and the top of the window. This can be accomplished by sliding a putty knife or trim pry bar

Nail holding in top of jamb liner

between the stop and the casing and then using a hammer gently, just like I describe in Part I of this book. Be sure to remove any nails that remain before proceeding. Save the stops and set them aside for later, because you'll reuse them.

Step 2 Prep For Removal

Open both sash halfway so that they are right on top of each other and you have an opening at the top and at the bottom. Check the top and bottom of the liner on both sides to look for a nail, screw, or just some caulk to make sure it is free from the jamb itself.

You may also have to cut free the paint lines between the jamb liner and the exterior trim if it has been painted over, which is often the case. Once you have freed it up on all 4 corners, you are ready for removal.

Bend the liner up and over the stool

Step 3 Remove Sash & Jamb Liner

It's time. Make sure to keep everything as one tight unit, because these liners are under spring tension and can shoot away from you if they are released without control. Put both sash in the upmost position and bend the bottom of the jamb liner up and over the stool at the bottom of the window on one side so that it can slide toward the interior of the building.

Once you get over the stool, you should be able to slide one whole side of the unit toward the inside and bring the other side with you. It will come out as one big unit of two sash sandwiched between the two jamb liners. Once you get it out, slowly release the tension on the springs and remove the sash from the liners.

How Install Jamb Liners & Sash

The installation process is pretty much the same process you did, except in reverse, but I'll walk through it briefly, because there are some slight differences you need to be aware of.

Step 1 Assemble the Pieces

Remember how it came out in one piece before? Well, that's how it has to go back in. You need to have both sash lined up and sandwiched between the two jamb liners with the small catch underneath each sash and the spring tensioned. Once you have your sash sandwich assembled, then you are ready to carry it over to the opening for installation.

Step 2 Install One Side at a Time

Put the bottom of one side into the jamb resting on the sill and slide the top into place. You'll next want to slide the top into place for the other side, and, just like during removal, bend the bottom of the last corner up and over the stool so that it can be pressed in place once everything is lined up properly.

Step 3 Install Stops

Once the jamb liners are in place and you've tested everything to make sure it fits well, then it's time to put the interior stops back on where they were using a couple 18 ga. finish nails. Caul the joints of the stops and touch up the paint if you need and you're good to go.

Install the sash as one big unit

Replacement Parts & Tips

Now we've talked about how to take things apart and put them back together again, there are a few tips about repairing or replacing missing or damaged parts that might be help to you. I've found that one of the most helpful sources for missing parts is Strybuc. They usually have what I'm looking for.

Overtime the vinyl can get brittle or other little parts can also break or require replacement and Strybuc as well as Blaine Hardware can be great sources for what you may need.

Spring Bolts

Spring bolts are one of my favorite alternative balances because they are just so darn simple. Spring bolts are a simple spring loaded metal bolt that is mortised into the side of the sash that protrudes into the jamb to hold the sash in place.

Typically, there is one on each side of the sash and two corresponding holes in the jamb where the bolts extend into to hold the sash in place either in the open or closed position. There are replacement spring bolts at a few online retailers like SRS Hardware if you need new ones.

If you are looking to install them on a sash that previously did not have them there are no modifications you need to make other than to drill a hole through the stile on either side of the sash and the have the corresponding holes drilled into the jamb.

Spring bolts are a great and inexpensive option for balancing a double or single hung window when there is currently no hardware or when there is no room for balance hardware like ropes and pulleys.

Installed spring bolt

CHAPTER 20
RESTORING STEEL WINDOWS

Steel casement and fixed windows are a very common historic window style. Big cities embraced steel windows early on to ease the fears of large scale fires that were common in cities in the late 19th and early 20th centuries.

Constructing windows from steel instead of wood became even more popular across America as the virgin forests that once covered much of the country were fast disappearing and the quality of wood was quickly decreasing.

Steel, on the other hand was one of America's great new exports and thanks to men like Andrew Carnegie, the price of steel was dropping significantly due to vastly increased production methods of the time.

Steel windows had a fairly short lived popularity in residential construction, lasting mostly from the 1930s to the late 1950s. But the end of that time period in America experienced tremendous growth in housing, especially after WWII.

If you have a home with steel casement or fixed steel windows, this chapter will help you repair and restore your historic windows. They are similar to wood windows in many ways, but different enough that they deserved their own chapter. Metalworking and welding repairs are beyond the scope of this guide, as they are usually out of the range of most DIYer's abilities, but you'll find most everything else you need to get your steel windows working and looking good again.

The focus here is on the materials and techniques to safely restore the appearance and workability of residential historic steel windows, though many of the techniques can easily be scaled to large commercial historic steel window installations.

MATERIALS LIST

- Roll of 3-6 mil. Plastic Sheeting
- Contractor Bags
- Trisodium Phosphate Cleaner (TSP)
- Respirator (N100 or P100)
- Safety Glasses
- Nitrile Gloves
- Masking/Painter's Tape
- Sharp 1/2" to 1" Chisel
- Pull Scraper (ProScraper vacuum scraper recommended)
- Sandpaper 80-grit, 120-grit and 180-220 grit
- Disposable Cotton Rags
- Disposable Chip Brushes
- Ospho Rust Treatment
- Sherwin Williams Kem Komick Universal Metal Primer (or similar product)
- Glass Cleaner (Windex or similar product)
- Whiting
- Spring Clips
- Sarcu Dual-Glaze (or similar glazing putty for metal surfaces
- Finish Paint (Oil-based recommended for metal surfaces)

TOOL LIST

- HEPA vacuum
- Hammer
- Glass Scraper Razor
- Angled Paint Brush

Old Windows In-Depth

Asbestos

Steel windows built in the 1920s-1950s occasionally contain asbestos in the glazing putty and caulk around the frames. Just like lead paint, asbestos is not something to scoff at. Before you plan to do any work on your steel windows, I would advise you to test for asbestos.

Unless you plan to remove the entire frame of your windows, there is rarely a need to disturb the caulk that holds the frame in place. However, if this caulk around the edges of the frame is cracking and falling out, it may need to be removed and replaced. If this is the case, have this area tested as well.

The Process

Just like with part I of this book, the process below is in a specific order that boils things down to the simplest and most direct route to restore steel windows. You can tailor any of this as you see fit, but after years of practice and honing this process, we have worked hard to pair the right materials and techniques to make the process go quickly and safely, and now you can benefit from all our trial and error.

> **PRO TIP**
> The order of operations is pivotal! It keeps things in order and you'll speed up the process and avoid rework.

STEP 1
PREP

Unlike wood windows, removing steel windows can be difficult, so for the DIYer, I recommend restoring them in place. With that in mind, keeping things contained and clean is even more important.

Proper preparation and planning will help you progress deliberately through the project and keep you safe. Be sure that your plastic is sufficient enough to withstand you walking on it and is wide enough to catch all of the debris that will be removed from the windows.

Action Steps

- Choose a calm day with minimal wind for your exterior work
- Lay down 4 mil. plastic sheeting within 6' of the window so that it will catch all debris. Tape plastic against wall.
- Wear safety glasses and P100 lead rated respirator at all times during work.
- Wash hands thoroughly with soap before eating or drinking anything on the job site. In general, do not eat or drink anywhere near the work to prevent ingesting any toxins.

Layout plastic and protect the area

STEP 2
DEGLAZING

A good technique to significantly cut down on dust is to use a spray bottle to wet the areas that you are working on first. A standard and inexpensive wood chisel works best. I recommend having a couple because they can dull quickly. The putty on most steel windows is too hard to remove with a putty knife. If you leave a little bit of remaining putty, it's not the end of the world, but you should have at least 90 percent of the old stuff off of the window.

Be aware of the spring clips. There should be one on the bottom (placed just off center) of each pane of glass and one on the top (the opposite side of center, usually). If the glass is in good shape, the spring clips do not need to be removed.

If you want to remove the glass, you certainly can, which will allow you to do a more thorough restoration; however, I have found it extremely difficult to remove panes of glass from steel windows without breaking the glass. Because of this, I recommend against glass removal unless the glass is already broken.

Action Steps

- Using a sharp chisel (and a hammer, if necessary) dig out the old putty, being careful to not break any glass or to gouge the spring clips that hold the glass in place.
- Remove any broken glass, saving spring clips. If the glass is in good condition, do not remove.

Chisel out old putty

STEP 3
PAINT REMOVAL

Paint removal can be easy or extremely tiresome, depending on how much and what types of paint have been applied over the years. Whatever the case, a good scraper will make the job much easier, and if you have one with a vacuum attachment like a ProScraper, you can virtually eliminate dust issues and really cut down on clean up.

Scrape everything down to bare metal. Be sure to open the windows and scrape inside of the jambs. This is very important. Your new paint will only adhere as well as what it is attached to. So, if you leave some peeling paint, it will continue to peel underneath and cause your new paint job to fail very prematurely.

Sand the surface smooth, being very careful not to scratch the glass. Then, vacuum up any dust and wipe everything down with a rag moistened with TSP to assure a clean surface before moving on to the next step.

Action Steps

- Remove all paint from any exterior metal surfaces associated with the window using a pull style scraper (with vacuum attachment preferred). Open casement windows and scrape jambs clean.
- Hand sand smooth all metal surfaces with 80-grit sandpaper first, then 120-grit sandpaper. *DO NOT SCRATCH THE GLASS WITH SANDPAPER.*
- Wipe down all surfaces of any remaining dust with a rag moistened with TSP cleaner.

Scrape old paint from interior and exterior

Old Windows In-Depth

175

STEP 4
GLASS PREP

You're almost done scraping! The glass will always have some remaining paint, putty, and gunk (not a technical term) stuck to it, which will have to be removed with a razor blade scraper. New putty and paint sticks best to clean glass.

Spray some glass cleaner on the window and scrape away. Wet scraping prevents dust creation and minimizes the risk of marring the glass surface.

Action Steps

- Wet scrape glass with flat razor blade to remove all putty and the residue.
- Clean glass with Windex and a clean rag or paper towel.
- For hazy glass that won't quite come clean, try CR Lawrence Sparkle. Buff on with a clean rag, let it dry, and then buff it off with a new, clean rag.
- Replace any missing spring clips. (See Step 6 for more information)

Scrape glass with flat razor

STEP 5
RUST TREATMENT AND PRIMING

Steel windows often have lots of rust on them, especially the bottoms. Ospho rust treatment turns iron oxide (rust) into iron phosphate, which is inert and can easily accept paint. This is an important step, because if you prime over rust, it will continue to rust underneath the paint and primer. Ospho is a phosphoric aside and is very caustic. It should be used with caution and all of the directions followed carefully. Do not get this on any glass, as it can etch the surface.

After the rust has been treated, apply a coat of metal primer. We use Sherwin Williams Kem Kromick Universal Metal Primer. Latex primer is not appropriate for this application. You need a solvent based primer since you are painting on metal. Try to avoid getting primer on the glass, but it's okay if a little gets on. You can clean it off later.

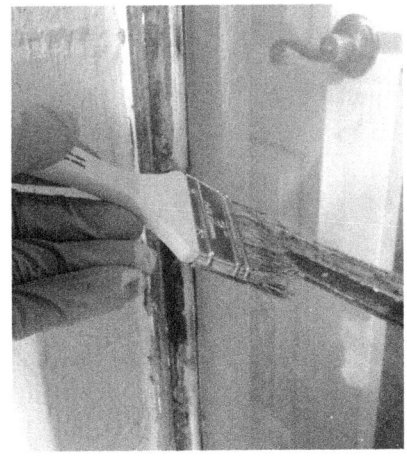

Apply Ospho rust treatment

Action Steps

- Wearing nitrile gloves and using a chip brush, apply Ospho rust treatment to all bare metal. Apply liberally to make sure all metal surfaces are coated, but do not allow to pool. Keep away from glass and painted surfaces. Clean up spills with water immediately.
- Wait overnight (8-12 hrs.) for Ospho to dry before applying primer.
- Apply one coat of Sherwin Williams Kem Kromick Universal Metal Primer to all exterior metal surfaces.
- Once primer is dry (approximately 2-4 hrs) sand _lightly_ with 180-220-grit sanding sponge. Blow off sanding dust using air hose or old paint brush.

Apply metal primer

STEP 6
GLASS REPLACEMENT

Glass replacement on steel windows is messy and often results in broken glass, unless you take hours to dig out the old putty bed. I prefer to put a tarp or canvas drop cloth outside in order to catch the broken glass shards. Slowly tap the old glass from the inside out to remove it. Make sure the spring clips are removed first, or you will be fighting them the whole time.

The glass will need to be sized slightly smaller than the opening so that it can accommodate the spring clips and not break under the pressure of the frame. 1/8" usually works.

Once all of the old glass is out, chisel out the remaining putty bed in preparation for the new glass. After you have placed fresh putty in the bed of the frame, install the spring clips and press the replacement glass into the putty to get a good air seal. One end of the spring clip will fit into a small hole in the frame and the other should rest on the glass.

Action Steps

- Remove broken glass by removing spring clips and gently tapping around edges of glass from inside with a hammer. This usually results in more pieces of broken glass, so, take appropriate precautions.
- Replace broken glass with double thickness glass cut approximately 1/8" shorter and narrower than opening.
- Back bed glass with putty.
- Insert spring clips to hold glass in place.
- Tool putty on interior to a smooth invisible line.

Install spring clips

STEP 7
GLAZING

Glazing windows is a bit of an art, and many require some practical to get lean, crisp corners, but with a little practice, you can do it.

We use Sarco Dual-Glaze putty, but you can use whichever type you would like or can find locally. Whatever you use, make sure that it is designed for metal sash and can stand exposure to the elements.

Action Steps

- Using a firm putty knife, apply Sarco Dual-Glaze to the glazing rabbets, pressing it into the metal and glass junction with moderate pressure.
- Tool glazing to a smooth finish with clean 90 degree corners. Remove excess putty.
- Using an old paint brush, apply whiting powder to outside of glass and work in thoroughly to remove oil spots from glass, being careful to not disturb putty. Whiting must be gently brushed into the faces of all putty to encourage skinning of over of putty.
- Using air hose, blow off remaining powder.

Apply putty in straight smooth line

Clean oils from glass with whiting

STEP 8
FINISH PAINT

The finish paint is how you protect all of the hard work you did, so pick a quality paint and apply it properly. I always recommend an oil-based paint for metal surfaces. It will provide a hard finish that will last years. Water and metal don't mix, so, a water-based paint may not be the best choice. Also, water-based paint has a tendency to remain tacky for a long time, whereas oil-based doesn't have this problem.

Make sure the paint is dry to the touch before closing the windows. For the first 30 days, I recommend either putting wax paper or vaseline in the jambs to prevent the fresh paint from gluing the windows closed.

Lap the paint onto the glass and be sure to paint these by hand. No spraying and scraping paint off of the glass. If you use a razor or tape to remove excess paint from the glass, you will break the seal that is protecting the putty and cause the paint and putty to fail prematurely.

Action Steps

- Once putty has skinned over (approximately 2 weeks) apply 2 coats of finish paint to exterior. Follow manufacturer's suggested drying time between coats. Allkyd (oil-based) paint is recommended on steel windows.
- Paint must lap onto glass approximately 1/16" to seal putty. Do not use blue tape or a razor knife to cut paint lines on exterior of glass. Exterior paint <u>must be cut in by hand only</u>.
- Place sheets of wax paper in moveable casement windows jambs to prevent windows becoming painted shut while paint cures.

Apply finish paint by hand

Old Windows In-Depth

STEP 9
INTERIOR RESTORATION

The steps to restore the interior of the window are much the same as the exterior, minus a few things. You won't have to do any glazing inside, and you should be more concerned with dust elimination to protect your belongings and family.

Inside, I recommend using a zip-wall system or making a bubble of plastic around the area you are working to contain the dust.

I've listed the steps below for the interior restoration below, but you can go back to the previous sections for more detail.

Step 1 Prep

- Lay down 4 mil. Plastic sheeting within 6' of window so that it will catch all debris.
- Using a zip wall containment system and 1 mil. plastic to completely encapsulate the working area around windows and protect against dust.
- Wear safety glasses and P100 lead rated respirator at all times during work.

> **PRO TIP**
>
> Consider upgrading the glass if you have the budget. Steel windows can accommodate more energy efficient glass like laminated glass or thick plate glass.

Step 2 Paint Removal and Sanding

- Remove all paint from any interior metal surfaces associated with the window using a pull style scraper.
- Hand sand smooth all metal surfaces with 80-grit sandpaper first, then 120-grit sandpaper. *Do NOT scratch glass with sandpaper.*
- Wipe down all surfaces of any remaining dust with a rag moistened with TSP cleaner.

Step 3 Glass Prep

- Wet scrape glass with flat razor blade to remove all putty and other residue.
- Clean glass with Windex and a clean rag or paper towel.
- For hazy glass that doesn't quite come clean, use CR Lawrence Sparkle. Buff on with a clean rag, let dry, then buff off with a new clean rag.

Old Windows In-Depth

Step 4 Pre-Treatment and Priming

- If inside of windows shows signs of rust, then follow directions above for Ospho pre-treatment. If there are no signs of rust, then proceed to primer.
- Apply one coat of Sherwin Williams Kem Kromick Universal Metal Primer (or similar product) to all interior metal surfaces.
- Once primer is dry (approximately 2 hrs.) sand *lightly* with 180-220-grit sanding sponge. Wipe away sanding dust with damp rag.

Step 5 Finish Paint

- Apply 2 coats of alkyd (oil-based) enamel paint to all metal interior surfaces allowing 8 hrs. drying time between coats (4 hours drying time for acrylic paints).

STEP 10
HARDWARE RESTORATION

Hardware on steel windows is extremely varied, depending on the manufacturer. Some windows are awning style, some inward swing casements, others outward swing casements. Whatever the case, a comprehensive discussion of all the specific hardware options and how to repair them would take dozens of pages of very technical and detailed instructions.

So, if you have hardware that needs repair, I have found there are three options that will resolve the situation.

Option 1 Clean Up

Sometimes it's as easy as removing years of built up paint and gunk (there's that technical term again) from the workings of the hardware. Scrape whatever paint off that you can and then on the more intricate parts, like gears, use a wire brush and some degreaser or cleaner like TSP.

Dry everything off well and add some lubricant like WD-40 or Dry-Lube and slowly try to get the gears working again. This is usually enough to get the function back and works for us to most of the time.

You can soak hardware in a crock pot like I discussed in Chapter 5 to get rid of decades of old paint as well should that be necessary.

Restored bronze hardware

Option 2 Reassemble

The other thing that may have happened is that the cranks have fallen out of place. Usually from getting banged by furniture or being forced to work when they were gummed up, the gears have come unseated.

If this is the case, you'll still want to clean everything thoroughly like I mentioned above, and then methodically take it apart and put it back together. Take pictures of everything as you do, so that you don't forget where something goes. Use the working cranks as a guide for how things should be assembled. You may be missing pieces, though and if this is the case, see Option 3.

Option 3 Purchase Replacements

Sometimes, the hardware is missing or too far gone to repair. If this is the case, you'll need to purchase replacement hardware. Depending on what kind of hardware you have, this might be easy to find or extremely difficult. Search architectural salvage yards, both locally and online. You can also try window parts companies like Strybuc, Swisco, Hope, and Blaine Window which have a wealth of different window parts specifically for steel windows.

Essentially, it relies on you to search the web for a part that will work. 20 years ago, this would have been almost impossible to find, but today, with the wealth of information online, you can usually find the part you are looking for.

CONCLUSION

I'm hoping that by this point, you feel pretty confident about rolling up your sleeves and tackling the window restoration process. You have the knowledge-tools you need, now it's time to pick up the actual tools that you might be lacking. Check out the appendix at the end of the book for most of the specialty tools you will need as well as the supplies I have available in The Craftsman Store on my blog. You can check back often, because we are always adding more products to help you.

Saving historic windows is a real passion to me, if you couldn't already tell. The beautiful design is what drew me to them initially, but their simplicity, repairability, and longevity is what keeps me coming back.

In modern society, they get a very bad rap. They are billed as the main source of problems for most old houses from high energy costs to water intrusion. They are viewed as evil, out-dated relics of a time when we just didn't know better. Nothing could be further from the truth. Our grandparents weren't naive to saving energy. You think the greatest generation that grew up during the Great Depression was wasteful? I don't think so! They were extremely resourceful and thrifty. Concerning windows, they used exterior storm windows because they knew their windows needed not only additional efficiency, but protection from the elements. Modern IGUs are based on this hundred year old idea of two pieces of glass with an insulating air space between them. They simply missed the part where the storm seals not just the glass area, but the whole window.

We've gotten trapped in a replacement mentality today where when a product wears out, we simply replace it. Part of this is laziness on our part, but the biggest contributor to this is the type of products available to us today. Costs have come down dramatically from a century ago and now it's rarely worth it to repair a product when the replacement is cheaper than the repair will cost.

Combine that with products that are designed to become obsolete or have a limited life before needing replacement, and you've created a vicious cycle of waste that is not sustainable long-term. Saving our built environment is the best way to save our natural environment and restoration is the cornerstone of this movement.

Restoration saves the things that are worth saving and makes them last the way they were intended. 50 years ago, restoration would have been the norm. It would have been expected and probably was simply called "fixing" things. But today, this simple act has become something radical. Something that normal folks think is the domain of only "hysterical preservationists" and tree huggers. How have we come so far from the expectation that you simply fix things when they break?

My hope with this book, and my blog in general, is to teach and encourage you to work with your hands again. To set aside those hesitations that you'll do it wrong or ruin something. Just get started! I guarantee you'll break glass, gouge wood, and break things that you shouldn't have, but that's alright. You're learning to fix things, right? It will take time and with each window you'll get better and better, faster and cleaner.

By simply starting, you'll learn a ton that I can't teach you in this book. You'll learn the feel of how much pressure to use and which direction to go with the scraper. You'll learn when your putty is too thin or too thick. Soon, the information in this book will just be the foundation that you build your restoration skills upon.

The time has come to put this book down and get to work. This book is a powerful tool IF you use it properly. If you read it and then set it on the shelf, you've missed the point. If after a few months the pages of this book are covered in dirty fingerprints, epoxy, and paint, then you have gotten your money's worth and you have made a difference. I hope you'll make a difference. I hope you'll get dirty. I hope you'll save your piece of history and that this book will help you. Good luck!

APPENDIX: WINDOW TOOL & SUPPLIES

What good would all this information without giving you access to the tools and supplies that you need. I've mentioned a lot of items in this book and so I felt that a recap of these tools and where to find them would be helpful.

The basic stuff like hammers and screw drivers you can buy anywhere, but for specialty items like glazing putty, vacuum scrapers, etc. you can find them all in The Craftsman Blog Store.

ProScraper

The bests scraper for windows that keeps your workspace clean and dust free by attaching to a standard shop vac.

Replacement Scraper Blades

If you're scraping lots of paint then you will probably need a replacement blades for your ProScraper. These double sides blades work perfectly.

Sarco MultiGlaze

The best all around glazing putty for in-shop use. Made from traditional ingredients like linseed oil and whiting.

Sarco DualGlaze

Best all-around glazing putty for steel windows and in-situ glazing which means you glaze your windows without removing them from the openings.

#1 Diamond Glazing Points

The most discreet and easy to hide glazing points for sash with small delicate muntins.

#2 Diamond Glazing Points

Big panes of glass need bigger glazing points and these can be easily driven by hand with the Glazing Point Setter unlike the #1s which require a point driving gun.

Triangle Glazing Points
Old fashioned glazing points that can be easily set with just a putty knife.

Glazing Point Setter
This tools helps you set #2 diamond points and triangle points with ease.

Samson Sash Rope
Famous for well over a hundred years this sash rope is both long lasting and attractive for any sash weighing under 150 lbs.

Whiting
Whiting is great for cleaning oils from glass after glazing and as an additive for your putty to help it reach a more workable consistency.

Spring Bronze
The longest lasting weatherstripping you can get. Lasts over 100 years and much easier to install the interlocking metal.

Coppered Nails
The nails you need to attach your spring bronze weatherstripping.

The Patinator
This solution is something I created to naturally add an old looking patina to new hardware to help it match the old stuff. No paint or coatings, just a true patina.

StopGap
An attractive way to seal up the draftiest part of old windows, the meeting rail.

Sparkle
A polishing compound for cleaning mineral deposits from old glass to make it shine again.

Speedheater Cobra
    It softens the paint in 1-3 seconds without scorching the valuable wood. It makes easy scraping of hard-to-reach surfaces with curves and details like old windows, spindles, and furniture. It protects our environment by eliminating flying chips and dust and uses approximately 75% less energy than the commonly-used heat gun.

Vintage Glazing Point Driver
    A completely restored vintage Glazing Point Driver! Pick your model No. 1 or No. 2 and your custom color to order. See the description below for information on the difference between the two model types.

Plaster Clamps
    100 extra clamps to use with the Plaster Magic system.

Plaster Magic Accessory Pack
    Some odds and ends to keep your plaster repairs rolling.

Patching Plaster
    This patching plaster is a dry, pre-mixed formula- just add water specifically designed for filling in holes in plaster with almost any substrate. It comes in a variety of sizes.

Plaster Magic
    Plaster magic is the best DIY way to repair cracked and loose plaster yourself. It comes in a variety of sizes.

StudPop
    The best stud finder on the market because it's simple, works every time, and is so inexpensive. It works on drywall, lath and plaster, and even on tile!

Spring Set
    The most accurate nail punch on the market doesn't even require a hammer. Set nails in any wood with ease and accuracy with a Spring Set.

Fletcher PushMate Point Setter
   Easy hand point setter for setting a variety of styles and glazing points.

Sparkle Glass Cleaner
   Referenced at least twelve thousand times in the book, here's the beloved glass cleaner for stubborn residue and stains to make old glass shine like new.

Made in the USA
Monee, IL
06 June 2020